Happily Single

After

FRANCHESKA M. PRICE

Happily Single After

ISBN 978-0692820421

Published by:

P.O. Box 8143 Pasadena, TX 77508

DEDICATION

I would like to dedicate this book to my mother, Helen Gray Price. You are my unvarying encourager, a true illustration of strength, and a model of resilience. It is my continuous anticipation and hope to one day be half of the woman you are. I can clearly recall times in my life where you have revealed to me the art of true womanhood. I will carry these lessons with me for the rest of my life, and will likewise instill this into my future daughters. I have watched you persevere while never giving up on God nor yourself. You have shown me how to truly be *Happily Single After* and I love you because of this!!

Lastly, I dedicate this book to every *single* person who has felt that their life was somehow lacking depth. I furthermore dedicate this to every woman that has endured unwelcomed circumstances but came out on top, nevertheless. This is for every person pursuing promise and purpose. Lastly I dedicate this book to everyone who has survived what was meant to break you. You are a survivor and you too will be Happily Single After!

ACKNOWLEDGEMENTS

I want to thank God for giving me the wherewithal to tell my story unapologetically and without trepidation.

I'm grateful for my grandfather, Alex Gray Sr., who told my mom over a year ago that I needed to write a book. Thank you for seeing something in me that I would not have seen otherwise.

I want to thank Bishop R.C. Blakes Jr., for helping me see who I am in God and to distinguish my value as a single woman. You are a blessing to me!

Special thanks go to my editor, Mical Roy. Thank you for dealing with my many texts and nervousness. You are a true artist and I value you!

Lastly, to Otis Spears, my graphic designer. Thanks for having vision beyond mine for the cover. I appreciate you for making all the changes little by little even for mistakes I made. You brought this work to life. My appreciation for you goes far beyond that which words can express!

Contents

Foreword

I am thrilled that Francheska has elected to sacrifice her privacy thereby forsaking her comfort zone to bear her soul to the world. When she came to me and told me that she was writing this book, I immediately knew that it was the mandate of God. Believe me when I tell you this author does not normally expose her life. This work is none other than divinely orchestrated.

It is the order of God's Kingdom that one must sacrifice him or herself for the rescue of a multitude. This book will prove to be a life preserver of those who read it. Though the author is an ordained and respected elder, she has put all of her holy garments aside to expose her deepest and darkest truths. She gives us what many authors are afraid of; she gives us her entirely candid and unafraid story.

In this work, Fran uses her pain as the foundation of a balm that will bring healing to the broken souls of many singles. She reveals secrets and vulnerabilities that most people would hide from the closest of friends. It is the unrelenting transparency on every page that grips the soul of the reader and applies the healing power through none other than truth and wisdom. The author takes the reader on her journey of singleness and exposes us to the pitfalls she's discovered along the way.

Francheska opens our understanding to the psychological locks that bind the single person to unproductive patterns and an inability to conceive happiness. She challenges the reader to enjoy the life that is presently their own.

While this book does get very emotional it's likewise a collection of life principles that every person may apply in an effort to avoid pitfalls while overcoming the many unfortunate situations that life often presents.

This is the journey of one who has been beaten and battered but never broken. This is the literary depiction of the author's journey to self-discovery and self-love. You will see that as she discovers herself, she additionally learns that the happiness she always sought was always within her and not in another. She's unapologetically *Happily Single After!*

R.C. Blakes, Jr.

Before ...

$\mathcal{C}$inderella is perhaps the most noted fairy tale princess of all time. Her life was on a downward spiral after the death of her mother. Her father became her everything but he subsequently married an evil villain we know as her stepmother. Cinderella was treated like a slave. She was required to work long hours and couldn't enjoy the pleasantries of her youth. Adding insult to injury, she sat back and watched everyone else seemingly succeed, and this left her single, alone, and dejected. It wasn't until she met Prince Charming that her life took a turn for the better and she received her Happily Ever After. Naturally, I am inclined to wonder how great her life may have been had she broke free from the words and actions of others and embraced being *Happily Single After* years of torment and pain instead of waiting on her Happily Ever After to enjoy that happiness.

One of my favorite artists of all times is the incomparable Anita Baker. Her music is such that it's both soothing to the soul and brings overwhelming ease to the mind. A particular ballad that I play continuously is called "Fairy Tales." This song outlines the paradox of love stories that our parents read to us versus the reality of a scorned love. In this song Anita Baker states:

"I found no magic potion, no horse with wings to fly. I found the poison apple, my destiny to die. No royal kiss could save me, no magic spell to spin. *My fantasy is over, my life must now begin!"*

Many of us grew up with fantasies of what love would be like and how our knight in shining armor would come and rescue us from a cruel world of being unloved. As noted in the song, many have found that the fantasies they were taught are not the reality they currently live. Some have been living in this realm of fantasies about love and marriage instead of facing the harsh reality that fairy tales happen in books but real life fairy tales sometimes come on the hinges of heartache and pain. A reality such as this often brings about much contemplation and is essentially a source of grief for many single people. These aforementioned feelings often cause us to miss out on being *Happily Single After* because we are so busy being Angrily Single After due to things not turning out how we might have dreamt they would.

YOU CAN BE SINGLE AND HAPPY!

Like Cinderella, single women have been taught to wait on Prince Charming and prepare for him instead of relishing happily in who God has created us to be amid this season of singleness. Society teaches us that in order to be happy we have to accomplish certain things such as having a great career, getting married, obtaining financial wealth and having children. Did you know that sometimes society can be wrong? Having these things is awesome but we as single people have to realize that even if we don't obtain these things, we are still FEARFULLY AND WONDERFULLY MADE! It's quite interesting that in Philippians 4:11 Paul speaks about a word we don't hear very often and that word is *contentment.* Just think of the beauty of your life when you fully operate in contentment with yourself and where you are in this life. You are enough! You are valuable just the way you are! You can be *Happily Single After*!

At the end of any fairy tale we read the words "...and they lived happily ever after." The truth is that we all have an after! What do we do when our "...and they lived happily ever after" is simply "...and *I* lived happily ever after?" How do we get to that point of acceptance of our single status, so that we can be happy and whole? How do we prepare so that IF God sends us a mate we can come to this mate complete instead of fragmented by the events in our lives that have caused us pain. How can we be happy when society shows us the picture of the blushing bride with a white dress and fabulous wedding? In this book, you will find the answers to these questions and more as I will candidly draw from my experiences and provide you with practical wisdom on being *Happily Single After*, all while you wait on your Happily Ever After!

Chapter One

Happily Single After Daddy Issues

A girl's father is often her first representation of a man. As her first love, it is her father that shapes and guides her into being the confident and gracious woman that she will eventually become. He sets the stage for any man that will enter her life concerning what she will or will not accept. As research has proven, a father is one that can make or break his children for years to come.

Growing up, my father was my WORLD! I could not see past him, which may have been because he was 6'3" in statue. I would get so excited when he would come home, primarily because I knew that no matter what time he came home I was going to go in his room, lay in his bed, watch what he watched and eat what he ate. I was the baby of five- three sisters and one brother- and at that time I felt that I was his world too. Until this day my mom swears he would feed me to ensure that she wouldn't poison him. He knew that she would never hurt her child but given the circumstances, she had every reason to hurt him.

Our household was filled with so much laughter, smiles and fun- all until my dad came home. As soon as he entered the driveway we became toy soldiers and those faces of laughter now became facades of fear. You see, my dad was tall in statue, carried a deep sultry voice and could be very intimidating to us. We didn't know if we would get the nice Willie or the drunken abusive Willie. It was often the latter. My earliest recollection of this abuse was when I was about four or five years old. My dad came home in a drunken state and instructed me to get out of the room. I remember seeing him push my mom on the bed during this process and he began to strike her repeatedly before I had a chance to remove myself from the environment. I remember this day like it was yesterday- even though it has been over 30 years.

My father was the definitive example of being a public success while simultaneously a private failure. He demanded respect wherever he would go and was the greatest charmer that I've met to date. He had a way with the ladies. Some would even say that he was a ladies' man. He was a socialite and would go to the local bars and order drinks on him for the house. At five years of age, I remember people asking, "Franny, where's your dad?" My response was, "Frontier Lounge!" Little did those at the lounge know that while he was buying rounds for bar patrons, my mother was at home figuring out where her kid's school clothes would come from or how she would get money to pay bills or even sometimes where we would sleep the next day. You see, by the time I was 18 years old, we had moved 16 different times- even in a shelter for battered women and their children- mostly due to an unstable man and his supposed dominion over our house.

My parents married in 1968, and nine months later they welcomed my oldest sister into the picture. They were 19, young and in love. Shortly after, my dad was drafted for Vietnam. His life was filled with disappointments stemming from having to drop out of high school all the way to desiring the good life on a limited budget. His life was one of non-completion by starting tasks without finishing them and wanting to look good in public while suffering on the inside. Alcohol became his vice and this would also become his ultimate undoing.

Around the age of 12, my relationship with my father endured a pivot of sorts. I begin to see who he really was as a man; thus shaping my view of men. The trauma of watching my mom continually abused by my dad and seeing the black eyes and scars from a man who claimed to love her is a trauma that I will never forget. According to an article on CNN entitled "Children, the Silent Victims of Domestic Violence," 10 million children are exposed to domestic violence each year. The article also states that there is a 30-60% chance that children who are exposed to domestic violence will ultimately be victims of domestic violence. Domestic violence harms children emotionally, physically and mentally. This is what it did to me as a daughter of an architect of domestic violence. From that age on I began to think that it was okay for a man to be abusive, aggressive, and unfaithful and that any man I would ultimately choose for a mate could carry those qualities and we could live happily ever after. Boy was this frame of mind wrong!

Maybe your father's vice was not domestic violence. Maybe his drug of choice was not alcohol. Maybe you grew up in a single-parent home and your father's struggle was that he was not there. For some of you reading this, you had an excellent relationship with your father but it was your mother who left you broken. I want to pause for a moment to let you know that *God is near and dear to the broken*. I don't understand why He allows good people like you to go through the things you did with your parent but what I do know is that He is protecting you even when you don't understand. Trust Him today!

Our view of fatherhood as single women is often shaped by the reality of who our father is. Bishop R.C. Blakes Jr., wrote a book entitled "The Father Daughter Talk" and one of the key points in the book is this quote:

"When a girl does not have the instruction of a father, she learns tough lessons in life through experiences. This often leaves her bruised, broken, and bitter."

The same can hold true for men who may be reading this book. Absent fathers may have created a space in a young man's brain of who and what he is to become and that male will fall into that often destructive path. Now, let's understand what an absent father is for future references in this book. An absent father is not necessarily a father that is absent from the home. A person can be with you but not be fully "present." When a parent is present, they are supportive, correcting, encouraging, and "all-in" concerning their child. I was sitting in a teacher in-service and I heard the speaker mention a story of a parent who had attended their child's tee-ball game for three years. The speaker began to say how the child wasn't a very good player but the parent was physically present at every game. One day the parent was sitting at the game and heard cheers coming from the audience and the person beside her began shaking her and asking her if she saw what had just happened. The parent noticed that her child had a huge smile and saw the team cheer but sadly the parent never saw the reason why because her face was submerged in Facebook. She missed her child score the winning goal! My friend, that parent was there but the parent was not "present."

Take a moment and think about how your father shaped your view of being *Happily Single After*. What issues from your childhood have been underdeveloped and underexposed? What hurt and pain are you carrying because of the fact that your father was a missing piece in your life? What mindsets are you holding on to because of the words spoken to you by your father? In this next section, I will uncover some of the mindsets that you may develop as a result of poor relations with your biological father. Understanding these mindsets will help to bring awareness to these areas in your life so that healing can begin. Let's expose some of those mindsets.

Mindsets From Our Fathers

If you want to know where a child develops his/her mindset and views it is often a good idea to point back to the parent. Likewise, if you want to know where an adult often gets their mindset/views it is a good idea to look back at the parent. As singles, we often carry the weight of things spoken to us and done to us by a parent. We enter into relationships with our unresolved parental relations that spill over into trust issues and a myriad of other things that often aren't easily traceable. Here are a few of the mindsets that affect us. When we understand and overcome these mindsets, we can move on to being Happily Single After!

Mindset 1: My father didn't want me so I am unwanted.

Rejection. Does this word sound familiar to you? Remember that time you were eavesdropping on your parent's conversation and you heard your father say that he never wanted you anyway? Or remember that time your dad favored your brother over you? This begins the mindset of rejection and the child begins to think, "I AM UNWANTED!" Maybe your mom told you of how your dad wanted you to be aborted but she chose to let you live. Rejection is both painful and shameful. Here is the problem with rejection. It makes a person hungry for approval and anxious to get that approval by any means necessary. That rejection could have led you in the path of rebellion against your parent. Maybe it drove you to the arms of an older man at a young age. It could have driven you to drugs. Did you become an overeater because of your rejection? For me, food was my drug of choice. As a kid, food was my connection to my father. This is what I used to combat the trauma from the events that I witnessed and the fact that my dad was there yet absent.

Guy Winch maintains several assertions in an article in Psychology Today entitled "10 Surprising Facts about Rejection." One assertion that he makes is that rejection and physical pain trigger the same region of the brain. He says that rejection can be relived and re-experienced more acutely than physical pain. What is this saying to us? The reason why you relive and experience the pain of the emotional trauma of rejection is because your body transforms this experience into physical pain. Think about the last time you stomped your toe. Can you still feel it? I sure can. Now think about the time when you were rejected? Can you see it, feel it and visualize it? I sure can. These stories that live in our head often keep us Happily Angry After!

Yes, angry because we have not dealt with the root of the rejection.

The root of many of the relational issues that we face is due to the rejection we experienced from our fathers. Why do you think that many have a problem with committing to long term projects and relationships? It's because rejection is embedded so deep and we often have not found a way to escape. *Rejection sends us on a self-destructive spiral that often ends with a wasted life.*

How do you end the cycle of rejection over your life? First, address it. What self-destructive behaviors do you engage in as a result of your rejection? Is it smoking, drinking, promiscuity, or even being an overachiever? All of these things are similar to the use of narcotics for physical pain as they mask a negative feeling temporarily; however, when the effects wear off we look for another fix! What's your fix? Today is the day you let go of your fix and move towards the power of completeness that can only come when you are free from the bonds of rejection! Listen, your God-ordained mate will not reject you! *You cannot be a happy single until the root of rejection is uprooted in your life and the seed of acceptance is planted.* Where will that seed of acceptance come from? Keep reading!

Even after you have acknowledged the root, you must now remove any negative thoughts related to your rejection. Thoughts such as "I am not good enough" or "I will always be rejected" have to become thoughts of the past. I used to place sticky notes all around my mirrors with positive quotes to help me when negative thoughts were present. You have to guard your heart and mind. There are times you have to turn off the television and meditate on positive thoughts. The Bible says in Proverbs 23:7 "As a man thinketh in his heart so is he." We often misquote this verse by saying, "As a man thinketh so is he." The bible clearly points out the term "in his heart." The difference is that when we talk about what is in our heart, we are talking about what is rooted and grounded even from the rejection you experienced from your father. The goal is being *Happily Single After* until you reach your Happily Ever After and unfortunately you cannot have the latter if you have not mastered the first and you cannot master the first until you remove the seed of rejection from your heart.

Mindset 2: I deserve to be mistreated by men because my dad mistreated my mom

As an adolescent, I thought that it was the norm for a man to abuse a woman. I even had thoughts at one point of wanting a man that would abuse me.

Sad but true. My mind was conditioned to accept what was happening around me as the reality of what would happen in a relationship. My self-worth was often a direct correlation of what was happening in my environment and this should have never been the case.

One thing that we do not talk about often in the Christian church is generational curses. A generational curse is simply negative mindsets, emotions, and behaviors that are passed down from one generation to the next generation. Have you ever heard someone say, "He's dealing with his father's demons?" In actuality, they are saying that he is dealing with a generational curse passed down from father to son. These are unresolved issues that need to be dealt with before they trickle down to your children or their children. Often the mistreatment of women by men is due to the male watching his father be a physical, mental, or emotional abuser. This is a generational curse. Often a woman being abused is the result of watching her mom's bout with similar abuse. This is another example of a generational curse!

Listen, just because your mom dealt with mistreatment doesn't mean that you have to. Just because this was the way things were for you growing up does not mean that it has to be that way for you as a grown adult. You deserve so much more than the experiences of your parents. Today, denounce every generational curse and mindset that is keeping you down. Begin to believe and trust God that you can have an abundant life and that the spouse that He has for you will not be a source of disrespect but he will love you as Christ loves you.

Maybe you are a man reading this book and you came from a womanizing home. You do not have to be this way. Often men tie their self-esteem to the number of women they can conquer. If you just trust God and know that as you do things His way He will honor you. Just because your father was absent, abusive, or cunning does not mean you have to be. Are you up for the challenge of being a better man than your father was?

Mindset 3: My mom did it without a man and so can I! I don't need a man!

Now, at this point, we may as well pull out the flute and harp because we have just heard the story of a woman who is Happily Angry After. She has not seen an example of a good man and because of pain she now says, "I don't need a man!" Guess what? SHE IS RIGHT!!

Modern day single women in America have been blessed with an opportunity to have it all. We can be your CEO's, lawyers, doctors and businesswomen and still come home, cook, clean, and have a social life. Money is easy to come by and we don't need to depend on a man for our daily needs. So, in essence, we do not *need* a man.

There is a "however" to this. The however is that often when a woman says that she does not need a man, it is not coming from a place of being a successful woman operating in an entrepreneurial spirit. It often comes from a place of self-sufficiency that she has developed as the result of poor relations with men. This woman develops the mentality that she will do it all on her own instead of choosing to realize the blessing that a man can bring to her life. As a result, the woman with the mindset of "I don't need a man" becomes overly aggressive and begins to take on the characteristics of a classical man. She becomes Alpha and "hard" as a result of the pain she has endured which has hardened her. I remember being hurt and carrying this mindset until one day I could no longer be hard and masculine. I realized that I wasn't created this way. I was created to be soft and loving. I began to pray and ask God to make me soft again and this is exactly what He did. He removed the stony part of my heart and gave me a heart of flesh. With that heart of flesh, I became more gracious and loving.

The woman who feels that she doesn't need a man is often aggressive and men are turned off by this aggression. She develops the mindset that she is still single because a man "Can't handle me." The issue with this is that it seems as if the problem is with the potential suitor when in actuality the problem is with the woman. *She must take a break from her high horse and be totally naked emotionally so that the layers of hurt can be removed.* If not she becomes toxic and hurts everyone that comes in her path. Listen, you cannot be Happily Single After if you have not let go of the mindset that you don't need a man. Am I saying that you wait and wait for this man or that your life is dependent on a man? Certainly not! But *when you build these walls you make it hard for the right one to cross over them.* I hear you say, "Well if it's of God he will just accept me the way I am!" The reality is that NOBODY has to accept you the way you are. We should all be on a quest daily for self-improvement and this quest begins within the delicate walls of our minds. *Being Happily Single After is about accepting that yes, I can do it alone but I am going to prepare myself so that I won't have to.* This attitude breaks down walls and barriers and opens the door to your Happily Ever After!

Mindset 4: My dad let me down so much so I will never trust a man

Remember that day that he told you he was coming to get you and he never did? Remember that time he was supposed to buy you a special gift and you never received it? Do you remember waiting on the corner for him to show up and your mom telling you to come inside but you refused because he said he was coming and he never did? Even as an adult you are probably feeling the pain of it even as you read this. This mindset trickles down from your childhood into your adult relationships. Trust!

Have you found yourself saying, "I will never trust a man?" You may have found yourself protesting by saying, "All men are dogs!" If so, then you are probably dealing with trust issues implanted by your father. Is this the case for everyone? No, but it is the case for many of us.

A mindset that does not allow itself to trust will ultimately spill over into your work life and home life. When your trust has been damaged by a father, you feel like you have to be in control of everyone and everything around you. *We cannot move forward as happy singles with mistrust in our hearts.* This mindset often leaves us alone and confused and we push others away because we simply refuse to trust. Being Happily Single After is a matter of understanding that we have to trust someone sometimes while realizing who to put that trust into. When we embrace trust then we embrace a new life and we are awakened to brand new opportunities daily.

Now that we have exposed mindsets we must now identify the ways in which we can be Happily Single After all of our daddy issues. *I want to make sure that you have practical steps on how to move to the next dimension of a happy life as a single person.* I will briefly outline three tools that will help us defeat and overcome any daddy issue that we face.

Begin to Know God as ABBA

Our view of God is often shaped by our view of our natural father. If your natural father was punitive and harsh, you may begin to believe that God is punitive and harsh. If your father was a loving individual, then you will view God as such. *We view God through the lens of our experiences and not from the fact of who He truly is.* When we have a negative view of who He is it pushes us further and further from Him and closer and closer to our "fixes."

In the Bible book of Mark chapter 14 and verse 36 Jesus says these words:

"Abba, Father, all things are possible for you. Take this cup from me; Nevertheless, not as I will, but what you will."

Abba is a term synonymous to "Daddy." It is a term of endearment and a term that lets the Father know that you need a special touch from Him that only a Daddy can provide. Abba is one of the most significant names of God as it points us towards the loving nature of who He is. Your natural father was simply "father" but God wants to be ABBA to you. He wants you to trust Him and even let go. He wants to be in the driver's seat in your life and show you what a true ABBA or daddy is. Will you let him?

Jesus was surrendering his total will to the will of the Father. To know God as ABBA you have to submit your will to him. What is your will? Your will is your mind and your emotions. You have to begin to seek the scriptures for verses on God's grace and mercy and how loving He is. You have to spend time in prayer even if it is little by little each day until you feel complete in Him. When you know Him as Abba your mindset begins to change. He begins to show you who you are and He gives you a new identity. You were once fatherless but now He is connecting you with a good Father! *Begin to cry out to Him by saying ABBA I need you to heal the holes my father left. Abba I need you to mend wounds that have been left open. Abba I need you!* Daddy listens. Daddy hears. Daddy loves! God has adopted you and He is ready to show you what a real daddy is.

Romans 8:15 "For you did not receive the spirit of bondage to fear, but you have received the Spirit of adoption by whom we cry out "Abba Father!"

Denounce negative words spoken over your life by your biological father

Dr. Masaru Emoto was a Japanese author who conducted various studies on the effects of words spoken over water crystals. What he found was that water crystals that were studied under a microscope formed into beautiful snowflake-like cells when positive words were spoken over them whereas water crystals that had negative words spoken over them formed ugly damaged-like cells. Our bodies are over 80% water so when negative words are spoken over us, this damages the cells in our bodies but when positive words are spoken over our lives the very core of our existence experiences remarkable modifications.

Think about the negative words spoken over your life by your father. I remember excitingly taking my dad my report card with all A's and B's. I was so amped to let him see it but he said these words when I approached him. "I don't want to see it if it is not all A's!" He refused to look at it. Although his intentions were good, his methods were not and this made me feel like I wasn't good enough. Maybe your father has told you that you weren't good enough. Maybe he has told you that you will never amount to anything. Denounce those words today. Take those words out of the atmosphere and replace them with the thoughts of ABBA! Abba says that you are good enough and that you were not a mistake! Begin to call out loudly every negative word implanted by your biological father and watch how the very core of your existence changes. We denounce them by not accepting them as truth. We denounce them by writing them down and searching the scriptures for everything ABBA says about you that is opposite of what your natural father says about you. This gets us closer to the Father and closer to being Happily Single After.

Forgive!

I have a confession. At one point, I hated my dad. I didn't care if he lived or died. I felt like my life would be better without him. When I was 18 years old I moved away from home for college because I did not want to be near him. We would argue and fuss and this became the gold standard of our relationship. How could I love someone who was at times so unloving and cruel? How could I love someone who allowed me to go to school with holes in my shoes or who would beat my mom to puddles of blood? Why couldn't I just have a "normal" dad? God spoke these words to me and it changed my thought process. He said, "I gave you the best father that YOU could have!" I was like, "Nope- you got that one wrong buddy!" Then He began to deal with me concerning comparisons. Our lives are not cookie cutter lives. They are uniquely shaped for our assignment. My father was the best father I could have for my life's assignment. Your father is the best father that you can have for the assignment that is on your life! I began to focus on the good times I had with my father- how I would come home from college and fall asleep in his bed to our "petty" arguments that would leave us both laughing and him saying, "You so crazy Franny!" *He wasn't perfect but he was mine.* I remember him being in the hospital in 2014 and him looking at me and saying, "The hardest thing I ever did was drop you off to college in New Orleans." He said, "I am proud of you!" I had never heard those words from him before and those words would be some of the last words I heard from him in life. A few months later on April 11th, 2015 my father suddenly died. I don't know if I had fully forgiven by this time. What

I do know is this. We can never let the sun go down while harboring anger and a spirit that doesn't forgive. You may be saying, "Well, you don't know what he did to me! He doesn't deserve forgiveness!" No, I don't but forgive him anyway. *Forgiveness liberates you!* You are reading this now and tears are forming in your eyes because you realize that you have to forgive. Yes, it hurts! No, they don't deserve it. YOU DESERVE IT! When you open up and forgive the sting of the past is released and you now become liberated by what has held your future hostage. **FORGIVENESS LIBERATES YOU!** You cannot be Happily Single After and harbor a life that lacks the ability to forgive.

Seek Out Fathers

In my quest to be Happily Single After my daddy issues, I had to seek out fathers. I had to seek out natural men who could help me identify what a real man looks like, walks like, and how a good man behaves. I began to lean on my pastor, a counselor that I trusted and other father figures in my life and they confirmed in me who I was in God and who I was as a woman. I remember meeting with the counselor and he said these words to me. "You are a quality woman!" These words shaped who I was and I stopped selling myself short of who God wanted me to be. God has given you men in your life as examples but it is up to you to lean on them. If you have no one, seek out books on fatherhood and scriptures on what a father looks like. These fathers will help shape you into being Happily Single After all of your daddy issues.

You do not have to be held hostage by the effects of daddy issues on your life. Maybe your daddy issue was not an issue with your dad but with a father-figure that you trusted. Today you have to be free from this in order to live a life of Happily Single After. *We can no longer hold on to the pain of the past because God's future for us is so bright.* Today I challenge you to release yourself from the issues created by your father. Allow yourself the opportunity to grow and blossom. Then and only then can you fully walk into your Happily Ever After!

Let Me Pray For You!

Father, I pray for the person who is reading this chapter today. I ask that you be ABBA to them. Show them that they are greater than any daddy issue and that they can overcome anything that comes their way. Lord, my sister needs you to wrap your arms around her. My brother needs you to reconfirm his manhood. Heal our mindsets today and continue to teach us how to be Happily Single After any daddy issue on this earth. We thank you for being a good Father!

In Jesus' name!

Amen!

Chapter Two

Happily Single After Mistakes

ave you ever met someone who has never made a mistake in their entire life? Me either! Each and every one of us has made some type of mistake. Some of us can make a mistake and move forward while others remain stuck in those mistakes. *The major problem with most mistakes is not the mistake in and of itself, but it's how we rebound from the mistake.* Someone is reading this right now and you are bound by an abortion that happened years ago. You are a hostage to past promiscuity. You have devalued yourself because something happened in your life and it has been a stumbling block for you. You will not be happily single if you do not embrace the mistake. We often hold ourselves hostage by the mistakes of our past. This is not God's design for your life.

Last year I had an opportunity of a lifetime to travel to Europe. One of the destinations was Rome and there we visited the Sistine Chapel. After viewing this historic landmark, we had an opportunity to tour St. Peter's Basilica which is viewed as one of the greatest churches in all Christendom. Inside of the massive and well-designed building, one will find tombs of past Popes. In one spot the tour guide instructed us to look at the floor. There was an iron circle on the floor and a light was shining from the ground through the circle. The tour guide stated that this is where the tomb of St. Peter is located. Here I am almost 2000 years after St. Peter died and I was at the burial site of a great Apostle, Preacher, Fisherman, and Disciple! What an honor! Stay tuned. I am going somewhere with this story.

This same Peter that people flock to see in a tomb every day is the same Peter that doubted Jesus. He asked Jesus in Matthew 14:28 to tell him to come or in other words to allow him to walk on water too. Jesus availed and then Peter began to doubt and started to sink. Yet another time Peter was being ridiculed for following Jesus and not only did Peter deny Jesus once but Peter denied Jesus THREE times. Peter was also known to be a man with a foul mouth. Yet in all these mistakes, we still travel thousands of miles to see the tomb of this Apostle, Preacher, Fisherman and Disciple and the only thing we remember about him at that moment is how he died for Christ! You see just like you and I,

Peter was bigger than his mistakes. His mistakes never disqualified him from being a history maker and Earth shaker- and neither do yours!

"Your mistakes don't disqualify you from being Happily Single After!"

Some of us are bound by our mistakes and shortcomings. Someone is even saying "I have had three kids out of wedlock so I am disqualified from being happy!" Another is saying "I have a criminal past so who would want me with this mistake?" The good news is that your mistakes do not disqualify you from being Happily Single After! There can be happiness after mistakes.

As a young child around the age of five years old, I was very precocious and inquisitive. This precociousness and inquisitiveness would prove to be a vessel used to pull me off course for years to follow. I remember at this age looking under a mattress and there was my father's Playboy magazine. I didn't quite know what I was looking at but it was something about it that made me become even more inquisitive concerning what my eyes had witnessed. This progressed to me viewing more inappropriate things even before I was 12 years old. It was readily available and something about it intrigued me more and more. As a teenager, I began to seek out the attention of men because of men due to the lack of attention from a father. I had a womanly body at a young age so older men were attracted to me. I would spend hours and hours on the phone as a 15-year-old with guys who were well into their 20's. The more I talked, the more I craved and talking then progressed into sexual activity. This was a mistake that I would regret and deal with for years to come. Sex became my "fix." When I was sad it was easily accessible. When I was in pain, it was what took the pain away- even if only temporarily. What I didn't realize was that the hole in my heart grew bigger and bigger with each encounter.

By the time I was 18, I was preparing to move away for college. Surely the demons of my youth would not affect the person I had become. You see, I moved to college at this time and I was well on my way to being a success. But when you don't deal with your demons they always resurface. My relationship with God grew stronger and stronger during this time but my relationship with pornography was an ongoing battle. I thought that since I did not deal with it every week or even every month that it was a non-factor when in fact it was a hindrance to my very being. I was young and ignorant of the saving power of Christ. Although at that time I had begun to study and teach the Word of God, I had still not given Christ total control of that area. No one knew- it was my secret thing. It was occasional so surely it was nothing to it right? Wrong!

As I grew in Christ I began to not like the person I had become. When you don't like who you are the natural thing to do is change and this is what I did. The reason why many of us suffer from a broken conscious with some mistakes is because we haven't really fully surrendered that area to Christ. I would have moments of surrendering then I would have moments where I gave in. Men would be my ultimate downfall.

At the age of 26, I was active in ministry. My joy was to serve others. By this time I was a homeowner and I was established for such a young woman. I met this guy that was well below my standards but he said the right things. Something happened that would prove to be an event that I would never forget. That something was that I became pregnant. Unmarried. Minister. Pregnant!! My brain began swirling. What would people think? What would my pastor say? How would this look? The father would curse at me and tell me how I needed an abortion because my pastor would sit me down and people would talk. Because of my "status", I made an appointment with an abortion clinic because this was an embarrassment that I could not face. I remember calling the clinic in tears because the weight of the situation was more than I could bear. Then a light bulb went off and I realized that the private pain of having an abortion would be greater than the public embarrassment of my mistake. It was then that I decided that I would keep my baby no matter what. Motherhood instincts and morning sickness began to hit. Then the shame of sitting in church being an unwed pregnant female minister began to weigh in my mind all the more. The stress of it all began to get to me. One morning I woke up bleeding. I lived alone so I drove myself to the hospital. While waiting on the nurse to take me to a room an older Caucasian guy was sitting next to me. He began to tell me how I had such peace about me and said, "You must be a Christian!" I was able to minister to him. Even in my pain, even in my mistakes God still had a plan and purpose for my life! I lost my baby that day but I regained my purpose.

I want to pause right here to let you know that no matter what your mistake is God can use you! God can use that mistake to bless so many others. Trust Him with that today. *Don't allow your mistakes to stop your purpose. Your mistakes don't push you away from the will of God. They push you in the direction of the will of God but only if you allow it.*

Your mistakes do not define who you are! You cannot be Happily Single After if you are constantly allowing yourself to be held hostage by the mistakes of your past!

The Twins that Define You

There are a set of twins that define you when you are living under the shadow of the mistakes you've made. These twins approach you like the shadow of death and suck every ounce of life from your body. They leave you breathless and hopeless and their ultimate aim is to leave you lifeless! They feed off of one another. Allow me to introduce you to the great twins called *GUILT* and *SHAME!*

Guilt is a feeling that comes after a mistake is made. It's often in the form of conviction. Guilt says, "I know I shouldn't have done that!" It's a quickening that can be used to keep us on track if we allow it. Guilt focuses on the behavior that you have acted upon. This feeling is often painful but it is a healthy awareness that there is a change in behavior that needs to be made. Unchecked guilt will make way for its evil twin that we call shame!

"Guilt is a feeling that I DID something bad. Shame is a feeling that I AM bad!"

Use your pointing finger to randomly point at an object. Now, think about what you noticed. You may have noticed that there was one pointing finger pointed to the object but there were three more fingers being pointed at you. Guilt is as the pointing finger that is pointed towards an object. Shame is like the three fingers that point back at you. Guilt is a feeling that I did something bad and shame is a feeling that I AM bad. Shame deals with how you view your personal character after a mistake is made.

Maybe you are holding the mistake of having a child out of wedlock over your head. Maybe you are holding the fact that you have dropped out of school against yourself. Shame begins to call you by your mistake. Shame looks you in the face and says "You dropout!" Shame says you're a divorcee so no one will want you again. Shame wakes you up in the middle of the night and calls you by the name of your mistake. You are so much more than your mistake! In order to be Happily Single After we must let go of the shame and understand our true character in God.

One of the roles that I have is as a Certified Belief Therapist. My goal as a belief therapist is to move individuals away from the lies that Satan has spoken to them and into believing what God says about them. It's a matter of replacing old mindsets with new mindsets. There is a new mindset that Christ wants to give you today. That is a mind that is free from shame. *Shame tells you that you are unworthy, inadequate and it condemns you. Christ says in Romans 8:1 that there is no condemnation for those who are in Christ.* Shame says that you will never change but Christ says in 2nd Corinthians 5:17 that you are a new creature. Old things have passed away and all things have become new. The only way to overcome shame is to seek the word of God and understand what He says about you and who you are in Him. It is time to let go of the shame today. Happy singles understand that no matter what mistake they have made, the shame of their past does not control the shape of their future.

The Twins that Should Define You

There is another set of twins that help us understand why we have the right to not live in shame. These twins are called Grace and Mercy!! They are the opposite of guilt and shame and they help us fully overcome them both. *Grace is simply unearned favor from God. It's when God does something for you that you did not even earn or have to work for.* When dealing with mistakes we have to understand that there is a level of grace that God gives us. Understand that this grace is not for something that has become a lifestyle but is shown on the coattail of mistakes. We cannot understand grace without understanding mercy. Mercy is when you don't receive the penalty for a crime you did commit. God is saying that yes, you had the abortion, you have been divorced but today I will not hold what you did against you. These twins cancel out the twins of guilt and shame! How awesome is that!

You may be asking how you can get over the mistakes you have made or how you can move on after a life of defeat. I want to tell you the three things you need to do to move away from your mistake and to embrace the freedom of being a happy single.

Repent

Oh no! She's using that word! There are some things that we have to simply ask God to forgive us for. 1st John 1:9 says:

"If we confess our sins He is faithful and just to forgive us our sins and cleanse us from all unrighteousness."

This requires some face time with God where it is just He and you with no distractions. *Pour out your heart to Him and ask Him to change your nature.*

Ask him to show you the root of your mistake and begin to pray against that root. Remember we talked about God being Abba? He is a Good Father that is waiting to hear from you.

Surrender

After you have repented to God, the next thing you have to do is surrender to Him. I mentioned earlier how I would go back and forth with the areas I struggled with. This was mainly because I had repented but I had not surrendered. Surrendering simply means to give God the driver's seat in your life. If you are like me, you like to be in control of every area of your life. *When we surrender we give up that control and do things the way He wants us to do them.* Happy singles understand that they are not in control of their destiny and they are content with allowing God to take the lead.

Forgive You!

I wrote about forgiving others in chapter one, but have you actually taken the time to forgive yourself? Yes, you were arrested at an early age and yes you've lied and cheated but this is in your past. Here's the hard truth. Whatever has happened in your life has happened. There is absolutely nothing you can do to change it. All you can do is press forward. *Forgiving yourself means taking the consequences that you impose on yourself out of the equation and moving forward with no regrets.* To be Happily Single After, you must embrace your past and forgive your failures. God has forgiven you so go ahead and forgive you too!

Your mistakes do not define who you are in life. They will not change God's intended plan for you. If He made you a promise then it will come to pass. Stand on His word and know that you can be Happily Single After any mistake you have made in life!

Let Me Pray For You!

Father, in the name of Jesus, I come thanking you that my brother or sister who is reading this prayer is moving beyond the mistakes of their past. I thank you that they will no longer walk in condemnation but in freedom knowing that you have forgiven them and your grace and mercy are covering them. Lord, we admit that we have made many mistakes but today we want to get it right with you. We thank you because no longer are we bound by the failures of our past. We declare that we are indeed Happily Single After every mistake!

In Jesus' Name!

Amen

Chapter Three

Happily Single After the Fairy Tale is Over

woke up this morning as a single, never married, childless, career-focused woman. Actually, I have awakened to this reality every day of my life. As a senior in high school, I took a Fine Arts Survey class and my teacher had us draw a shield. The shield was a representation of our future and the life we dreamed of having. On my shield I drew that I wanted to attend Dillard University or Xavier University (I am a Bleu [Yes, B-L-E-U] Devil- Go DU!), that I was going to have a Camry or a Lexus, and that I was going to be married and have my 2.5 kids plus a dog. Well, 18 years later I can say this- I am certainly enjoying being a mom to my miniature poodle. You see life has a way of making the personal fairy tale that we create in our own mind seem as if it is an ultimate reality.

What do you do when the life you dreamed of does not line up with the life God has you currently living? What do you do when you have worked hard to build your dream and it seems that what you have built will not work out? What do you do when you are now well past the age you desired to be married and you are still single? What do you do when you wanted the husband and the kids in that order but it seems that the order was reversed and the aforementioned is not in sight? What do you do when the fairy tale is over? The answer to these questions is...

YOU WAKE UP!

Listen, the reality is that for most of us the life we planned is not the life we live. You cannot be Happily Single After if you are holding on to the life you had planned while forsaking the life you HAVE!! Where you are is where you are and where you are going is where you are going! You have to accept where you are to embrace where you are going. *Many of us are walking in a sea of disappointment and live in the realm of the agony caused by disappointments. Here's the reality. We are only disappointed by our own expectations.* This is true in life and relationships. I want to snap you into your current reality. I want you to realize that no, this is not the life you planned but yes, you can still have an amazing life! I want you to be FREE from your fairy tales and embrace the reality that you can be Happily Single After- even after the fairy tale has ended, and even if it is not the ending that you had written so eloquently about yourself.

Sleeping Beauty Arise!

There is a popular fairy tale about a Princess dubbed Sleeping Beauty. Her mother, the Queen, had hoped and wished for a child. This dream for the mother seemed as if it was something that would never happen until a frog came to her and told her that she would deliver a girl within a year. Indeed, a year later she gave birth to the most beautiful Princess in the world and this captured the King's heart. It would seem as if Sleeping Beauty's life was going the way her parents and even she had dreamed for it to be but this would all be delayed because of a setback by an evil Fairy that cast a spell on her. Finally, a prince came kissed her, she awakened, and within one month they were married and they lived Happily Ever After.

Many of you are wondering where is the fairy that will wake you from the seeming spell that has been looming over your life and deliver you to your Prince! You are wondering how long you have to lie in wait and hope for your Prince to arrive so that you can get to your Happily Ever After. Listen, *your Fairy will not show up until you harness the power that is on the inside of you* and wake up to the reality that in this day in age...

YOU ARE YOUR OWN FAIRY!

As singles, we have often slept on ourselves and our dreams because we are waiting for the perfect opportunity to start life. I was meeting with a young lady about working with me on a business venture. This young lady was highly successful and had the world at her hands. I began speaking to her about home ownership and the benefits thereof. She said these words to me and it totally shifted my view of how our mindsets develop as singles. She said, "I can't buy a house until I get married. When I meet him, he should have a house and then I don't want to have to deal with two houses!" You should've seen the look on my face! Here is the fairy tale: I will meet a man and he will have it all together. Then I can work on getting myself together based on what he has accomplished and we will live Happily Ever After! Here's the reality. More than likely you will be an established adult before you meet Prince Charming and you will have to get yourself together before he comes. Sleeping Beauty, it is time to wake up from your slumber and realize that life doesn't happen as planned but life happens according to God's purpose and plan for you. It's time to stop sleeping on you. Sleeping Beauty, it's time to arise!

Stop Trying to Fit Glass Slippers and Start Breaking Glass Ceilings!

I began this book talking about Cinderella and her quest for Happily Ever After. We often focus on the process of Cinderella but it's another group of women in the story that I would like to mention. I began to think about the women who lined up for miles and miles just to take a chance at trying to fit into this glass slipper. I began to think how these women put their destiny on hold just for an opportunity to try and obtain their Happily Ever After. Then I started to think. What happened to all the girls who couldn't fit the slipper? Did they feel like they had missed destiny? Did they look for another man immediately? Did they fall into a depression because the life they dreamed had turned into one big ball of disappointment? I began to think about these women and what their plight was afterward. Then I was brought back to Cinderella. I thought about how all these women were chasing the slipper but the one who the slipper was designed for was at home chasing purpose and Prince Charming eventually rediscovered her.

So it is with many of us. We have chased our Happily Ever After so much that we have forgotten to be Happily Single After in the process. Let me ask you this question. This question is a question we don't like to talk about but it is very relevant. What if your Prince Charming never comes? What will you be able to say you accomplished in your life while NOT waiting for someone to change your marital status? Here's the reality. According to a Pew Research study, the marriage rate for those over 25 years old is lower than before. By the time this group is middle-aged, 25% will have never married. What if you are a part of this 25%? You may be thinking that this is a negative confession but this is ultimately the reality. Your plans may not be God's plans for you and what will you do about it? Proverbs 16:9 (New Living Translation) states:

"We can make our plans, but the LORD determines our steps."

It is God who determines your set time but it is you who decides what you do until your set time for Happily Ever After comes. Our goal as single women is to stop trying to be the perfect fit for a man and start being the perfect fit for our individual assignments! *While Ruth was waiting on Boaz she was working in the field. Her mind was far from a man but on her assignment.* It was while she was operating in her assignment that her Man of Purpose was revealed. There is a glass slipper that only you can fit but if you never step out of the glass slipper mentality you will never shatter glass ceilings!

Do You Have the Other Slipper?

I recently had a conversation with a male friend. He is 45 single, no kids, never married, six-figure income, drives a Porsche and lives in a gated community. He has finally reached the point of settling down but his chief complaint was that women that he considered had nothing to bring to the table. You may say, "I am a good person so my Prince should accept this!" Baby (in a deep New Orleans accent) it takes more than this to have something to bring to the table. What self-improvements are you doing? How are you maximizing your single life? What assets are you currently building for yourself? Do you have the other slipper?

You may be wondering what I mean when I ask you if you have the other slipper. When Prince

Charming rediscovered Cinderella, she had something that he was missing. She had something in her possession that no other woman could give him. She had something that was unique. That something she had was her glass slipper and it set her apart from anybody else. Let's go back to the Garden of Eden. God took from the rib of Adam to create Eve. Eve had something that Adam was missing. She had something that no other woman could ever have. This is how we have to be as singles. *We have to have something different that no one else has but that will be immediately recognizable by our future mate. You have to become what you want. If you want a man that is successful, you have to become a success.* Modern men are looking for a woman who can complement them and not the typical woman who will stay at home and live off his success. We are living in the age of power couples. What power do you bring to the relationship? Sure, the man you want is powerful, but do you have the other slipper? Do you have in you the very thing that he is looking for to bring completion to his purpose and destiny while fulfilling yours?

You may be thinking that you haven't met him yet and you don't know what type of slipper will be the best fit for his life. The type of slipper that will best fit his life is when you become all that you have been purposed to be and you walk in what you have been purposed to do. *It's only when you stop chasing these glass slippers and focus on destroying glass ceilings that your Prince Charming will enter and your life will go to another level.*

Living Life on Purpose

What is your purpose? What is the very thing that you have been destined to do that no one else can do? What is the improvement of a current concept that you have been thinking of accomplishing for a long time? Why are you alive? Happy singles seek purpose more than glass slippers. They know they cannot sit idly and wait for a person to complete them. They allow their purpose to complete them! That purpose can be found in two places- your pleasure or your pain!

What is it that brings you pleasure and you can see yourself doing for free? How could you harness this pleasure and create a business from it? Do you love to dance? Are you an excellent cook? Do you love to counsel people? Maybe interior design is your niche. When your pleasure becomes your passion then great things can happen. Happy single women know what brings them pleasure. They know that these things fuel their purpose and they constantly seek them out daily to find ways in which their pleasure can fuel their purpose. In order to be Happily Single After, we must unleash our pleasure to the world and allow it to work for our purpose.

In the next chapter I will talk extensively about pain and share with you candidly from my own personal pain. I want you to take a minute to think about the thing in your life that has pained you. Now imagine yourself using this as a platform to help other people who are in the same situation as you. Maybe you were like me and grew up in an environment of abuse. Your purpose may be to build a shelter for victims of domestic violence. Your purpose is a unique solution that only you have to meet the needs of multiple people. You see, for some people, their pleasure is the ultimate purpose predictor, but for others, your pain is the ultimate gauge of your purpose. *Too often we are scared to use the power of our pain to help others. When we do this we fail to realize that the power of pain can be broken by the releasing of our story to those who are going through a similar fate.* What portion of your pain is driving you to purpose?

One of the common themes of women who have been married for quite some time is that they lose who they are. The purpose of being Happily Single After is to ensure that when your time comes for marriage you will be full and complete and know who you are. This will foundationally equip you not to lose yourself in your marriage and to consistently be the person your future spouse will always need. When my parents ultimately divorced after 35 years of marriage, my mother went through a very tough transition. She had been married since she was 19 years old and now she had to discover who she really was. She spent her life raising her kids and catering to her husband. She did not even know what her favorite color was. In the process of helping everyone else, she lost herself. When we become happy singles we safeguard ourselves from losing our very identity at the cost of marriage. The cost of marriage? Yes! When you get married there will be a constant dying to self that has to take place. When you embrace and know who you are beforehand the foundation is set for the rest of your life and you can seamlessly balance both worlds- the "you" and the "marriage."

Let's Shatter Some Glass Ceilings!

Hillary Clinton recently made history as being the first woman to be elected as the presidential candidate for a major political party. On the night of her acceptance speech, the crowd stood in amazement as a video began playing. In this video, one can see the images of several past presidents. You see the likes of Abraham Lincoln, George Bush,

Barack Obama, and even Ronald Regan. Then, as the screen pans out, you hear a loud breaking of glass and a shattered screen could be seen on the video as a picture of Hillary Clinton emerged. You see, presidential hopeful Hillary Clinton realized that although this had never been done before, it could possibly be done through her. Although she did not win the election, she didn't have to wait on her husband to make things happen for her but she began to make things happen for herself. She knew that the present circumstance was not an indicator of her future destiny.

A glass ceiling is the limitations that we place on ourselves as singles because we are still living in the fairy tale of Happily Ever After. A glass ceiling is when you say, "I can see myself getting there but only if I had a better career." "If I had a husband I can do that," or "If I had everything I need then I can be successful." We wait, like the woman who did not want to purchase the house, for an opportune moment or a man to save us from what we deem as impossible situations- not realizing that all along, the power was in us to obtain greatness. Often when we think of glass ceilings we think of the business world and climbing the corporate ladder but there are some other glass ceilings that we need to break in order to live Happily Single

After until we become Happily Ever After. It's time to start breaking some glass ceilings!

There are three things that hinder us from breaking glass ceilings in our lives. When we overcome these three things as singles, we can truly embrace the concept of being Happily Single After. If we don't embrace them, we will live our after in a sea of dreams while watching others become their own fairy.

Competition

Remember the women who lined up for miles and miles simply to have a chance to attempt to fit the glass slipper that Prince Charming carried? All of them knew in their heart that the slipper they were trying on would not be a match because the slipper was designed to be worn by one woman and one woman only. So it is with us. We have been guilty of trying to fit into a space that is not our own space but it was designed for someone else. You cannot live Happily Single After and have a life of competition with other women to succeed in life. **You are not your sister's competition, you are her complement!** We have to move away from the feeling that we have to be in competition with another woman. Yes, I know the ratio of men to women is scarce but *what I know more than that is* *that what is for you is for you and no one can snatch this out of your hand.* As women, we compete far more than we complement.

Think on this. All of the women in line to meet the Prince knew the slipper would not fit but they tried anyway. Let me add a peg here. Some of you are dealing with members of the opposite scx that you know are not a good fit for your life. Maybe they are married and you are single. That's not your slipper! Maybe he is emotionally unavailable or leading you on. That is not your slipper! Your slipper is uniquely assigned to you and it will be in a space that no one else can claim. Go after your own slipper and leave your sister's slipper alone!

What if all the women would have rallied together to help Cinderella reconnect with the Prince? What if they weren't so intimidated by who she was but they understood that what God is doing for my sister He can also do for me. You see, when we align ourselves with another sister who is walking in purpose or is forming then we, in turn, will be blessed because of it. What you make happen for someone else, God will make happen for you. If the women had shown support for Cinderella's dream then ultimately she would have gotten to her dream faster and she probably would have reached back and hooked them up with another Prince. When we help our sisters get to where they are going then we create space for them to help us get to where we are going.

But I don't do women! Yep! You know you've said this a million times. We say this because often the intimidation from female to female is extremely intense and we have been lied on and talked about by our fellow sisters. This is why you have to surround yourself with women who are headed in the same direction you are headed in. *You have to seek out mentorship from another sister who is doing what you want to do and will ultimately go where you want to go.* As you push and support her vision, God will make room for yours to shine.

We have become severely accustomed to dysfunction as women and we think it's the norm. Watch television on any given day and you will find a reality show with women bickering and fighting aimlessly, continuously, and pointlessly. They walk around in a cloud of confusion, primarily because the life they wanted is the life they see someone else with, not realizing that if they support their sister, they can obtain the same thing. *We are more powerful together than we are apart. We need other women to help fulfill our vision. Women who are Happily Single After understand the power of connection.* They understand that as I rise and lift my sister up then she will rise and lift someone else up. They realize that their sister is a conduit to destiny and not a competitor for destiny.

I have three natural sisters and I am the youngest. At one time we all shared the same room and inhabited the same space. Did we have disagreements? You bet! But one thing we have never done was compete with each other. We know that as the other grows so will the rest. We respected the space of each other and recognized and celebrated our individual and collective success. We knew that each of us had our own glass slipper and if we wore the slipper that was uniquely ours then surely we could break any glass ceiling that was hindering our progress. We knew that if we bonded together to help the other shatter a glass ceiling then the way would be paved for us and we can join forces together to help us break even more. *A Happily Single After woman is not a woman of a jealous spirit. She is a supportive woman that will go out of her way to make sure that the women around her operate in their full potential-even if she is not currently operating in hers.* She awaits her turn and has an attitude of servitude towards her fellow sisters because she knows this will help her be Happily Single After while she is waiting on her Happily Ever After.

Comparing

A Happily Single After woman knows the value of not comparing. She understands that the life she has may not be the fairy tale she planned, but it is the best life SHE could have. **There is no one that compares to you!** Think about that for a second. At first, it may sound arrogant and a bit cocky but when you think about it, no one can compare to you. You are fearfully and wonderfully made in the image of God. No one on this Earth has your DNA. No one can walk in the gifts that only you possess. Therefore there is no one that compares to you. Theodore Roosevelt once said, "Comparison is the thief of joy!" When you compare you cannot be Happily Single After because your joy is stripped and you now look at your life as more than what it is or less than what it could be.

Comparison says, "My life is harder because I have a child and I'm a single mother." It says, "She has it easier because she has a husband and I don't." Comparison robs you of your uniqueness and causes you to reluctantly lose your gifts. When you compare you admit to being inadequate and incapable of your life's assignment. On the flip side, comparison causes you to be judgmental of others. Comparison says, "I am prettier than she is!" It says, "She overweight and ugly so how did SHE get a man and I'm still single?" Judgmental comparison brings with it a feeling of entitlement due to the fact that we have made it to a particular level so we feel should have certain things. I remember my thought pattern brought me to the point of saying, "Well I am single, educated, a great cook, I clean and I have no kids. I just don't understand why I am still single and so and so just got married and she doesn't match my qualifications." Now, how judgmental is that? Instead of celebrating with other women I became a hater of other women and could not celebrate the blessings of another because of what I deemed burdens of my own life. A happy single woman knows that she can't put herself down to make others look good and conversely she cannot put others down to make herself look good. She understands that in order to be Happily Single After, comparisons cannot and should not be made because there is no one that compares to the greatness on the inside of her.

There is one time that you should compare. This time is when you are comparing who you are now to who you want to be. It's when you compare your present life to your promised life. In order to be Happily Single After, you must always be on a mission of self-improvement. I can recall starting this year off depressed and suicidal. I looked in the mirror and I realized that I didn't like the person I had become. I was 263 pounds and counting and it seemed that my life was on a downward spiral. I could blame life's events for my spiral but I understood that the power was in me for change. So I put on my big girl panties and did something to change. I compared where I was with where I wanted to be. I got off my butt and DID SOMETHING!! It should be this way with you. You must get off your high horse and do something. If you want to be great, get up and make great happen! *Listen, the person who is walking in what you ultimately want to walk in is no different than you. The only difference is that she took a leap of faith and walked out on the very thing that she knew she was created for.* A Happily Single After woman understands the power of the moment and that she doesn't have to compare her life to others but she can use her present situation as a gauge to dictate where she will ultimately go.

Complaining

Joel Osteen said, "If you cannot be positive then at least be quiet!" I cannot stand to be around a person that continually complains. If you find yourself complaining more than you are finding yourself being grateful then you are living a life of Miserably Single After! Sure, your fairy tale did not happen the way you planned but let's be real for one moment. Most of where we are in life is a result of the decisions we have made with our life. You can complain about being a single mother but in most cases except being a widow and some divorces, this was a decision that was made. Yes, our decisions take our lives beyond the fairy tale that we envisioned, but it is what our life is now. When you complain, you are not living in the now. You are living in the fairy tale land of your own desires which may not line up with your ultimate purpose. In order to move from Happily Single After into Happily Ever After, we must let go of the spirit of complaint and change the things we want to be changed in our personal lives and in our surroundings.

Look at this scripture in Proverbs 30:21-23 (NLT).

"There are three things that make the earth tremble- no four it cannot endure: a slave who becomes a king, an overbearing fool who prospers, *a bitter woman who finally gets a husband,* a servant girl who supplants her mistress."

Did you catch the third thing? A bitter woman who finally gets a husband! Complaint is a form of bitterness that can be carried from your single life to your married life. This verse originally states the odious woman. Odious means unpleasant or repelling. Commentators state that she did not display these characteristics when she was single but as soon as she got married she became a complaining and repulsive woman. She was a bitter complainer as a single woman but concealed this and her true colors came shining through once she became a wife. Who you are now will dictate who you will be while you are in your Happily Ever After. *Happy single women wake up each morning with an attitude of gratitude. They meditate day and night on positive thoughts and allow the negative thoughts to whittle away.* Happily Single After women choose to change their surroundings instead of complaining about their surroundings. Today don't allow complaining to hold you under the glass ceiling of your destiny. You will be better off without complaints.

Embracing Your Reality

You have to let go of the fairy tale and the way you envisioned your life to be to embrace the reality of who and what you really are in this season of your life. *Remember that you are your own fairy! You can, by your actions and obedience to God, live the life you always wanted and be single at the same time.* You have to offer the other slipper to Prince Charming when he arrives. You are a solution to his problem but you are also a solution to another sister's problem while you are living in your Happily Single After. The only person you can compete with is you. Don't waste time trying to fit the glass slipper of another. Just be you on purpose! God is writing your love story. In the meanwhile begin making sure all the details of your story are handled and that you are a Woman of Purpose who is destined for a Man of Purpose. Let go of what didn't work and the life you envisioned for your current stage of life and embrace the life you have so you can have the life you always wanted. Anita Baker made this so clear in the song "fairy tales." She said, *"My fairy tale is over my life must now begin."* God is writing your love story. Trust Him with the pen!

Let Me Pray For You!

Lord today we trust you with the pen in our lives. No longer will we live in the bubble of a fairy tale but we will live out our reality and your plan. Thank you that there is more to life than a glass slipper. Thank you that today we are breaking glass ceilings. We promise that while you are holding the pen to our story we will not compete, we will not compare, and we will not complain. We love you and thank you!

In Jesus' Name!

Amen!

Chapter Four

Happily Single After Pain

After graduating college in 2002 I enrolled in seminary to pursue a counseling degree with biblical emphasis. This was a tumultuous and turbulent time for me as I was no longer living in a dorm so bills were now a standard. I was going to school from 8:00 a.m. to 2:00 p.m., working job one from 3:00 p.m. to 10:30 p.m. and then going to job two from 11:00 a.m. until 7:00 a.m. It was a rough transition but I was determined to make it happen at any cost. I was mentally and physically exhausted! I remember one night going home and praying to God from the depths of my soul concerning three things. I told God that I was lonely, I needed a financial breakthrough, and I needed to know that someone was praying for me. I arrived at school the next day and went to class. My classmates handed me an envelope. They had collected over 200 dollars for me. Next, one of my classmates told me that I was in her prayers all weekend. God was truly on a roll with answering my prayers that day!

Then seemingly out of nowhere this tall, handsome and athletic guy showed up and asked where I was going and hopped in my car and went with me. I had seen him around campus a few times and he was a sight to behold. He was smooth with his words and had a cockiness that was so attractive. He was a budding preacher and his ambition was through the roof. My self-esteem was at an all-time low and I was enamored by the fact that someone "like that" could show interest in an overweight girl like me. After a few weeks I begin to see that everything that glitters wasn't gold and certainly he was far from it. Inconsistency became his hobby and a womanizer became his character. A few months later he became the college minister at a campus near our seminary. This was also when I found out that while he was pursuing me, he was engaged to be married and would subsequently get married a few months later. The shock and disappointment I felt were far reaching but I dusted off my wound and kept kicking. I realized that, as the old folk would say, sometimes the devil hears your prayers too! What I thought was an answered prayer was actually a major distraction from purpose.

I never forgot him in the years to come. Time would pass and more relationships would develop. Let's fast forward to June of 2013. It was eleven years later and now Facebook had become a thing. I discovered that the man who stole my heart and also broke it had been divorced for two years and was back on the market. We reconnected and he told me about his divorce and how God had changed his life since then. It seemed that his marriage was over because his womanizing ways took a toll on the marriage. He lost a campus ministry of over 300 students that he and his wife were pastoring. For him, it seemed the pain was so deep and he swore he would *NEVER* cheat on another woman again in life. He sounded so sincere and I believed every word that came out of his mouth.

At this point, a long distance relationship ensued. We lived about 500 miles away from each other but I visited him every three weeks. Something in me kept telling me to run but the soul ties we developed ran deep. He became emotionally needy and since I thought I could save him I allowed him to be dependent on me financially, spiritually and emotionally. We began to get prophecies in just about every place we went about how God would use us in marriage. When hard times would come I clung to these prophecies because surely this was the will of God for my life. In July of 2014, I would find myself being needed again as he would enter ICU for several days and I flew there to ensure his every need was met. It was during this time that I became one of the happiest women in the world because he would go on to ask me to be his wife! Mrs. HIM!! The man I labored for and worked for. He had finally chosen ME!! It was finally my turn!! He was moving to Houston to be with me! I was going to walk into my Happily Ever After! So I thought!

A Meeting with Pain

Wedding plans were being made. My dream dress that fit in all the right places was purchased. The venue was booked and I had the best decorator in Baton Rouge ready to coordinate and provide décor for this auspicious occasion. My 13 bridesmaids had begun purchasing dresses and the stage was set for a night to remember. Then on January 15th, 2015, I received an invitation to a meeting. This meeting would be one that would change the entire scope of the life that I had grown accustomed to and the life I was about to have. My meeting began at 11:00 p.m. This was an impromptu meeting that I had no prior knowledge of but I had seen the face of the inviter many times before. Now I know you are asking why I would go to a meeting that late in the night. I will tell you briefly. I went to bed around 9:00 p.m. as usual and at 11:00 p.m., I was awakened to a text message. Seeing that it was from the man I was scheduled to marry less than five short months, I excitedly checked the phone. As I opened the text, I see a picture of him asleep and naked in a woman's bed with a caption that read, *"Don't ask me why but since you two are talking about marriage, I just thought you should know how he really spends his time. I'm enjoying the sex for now but hey- at least you know. Best wishes!"* Immediately I knew this was a meeting I wanted no part of.

This meeting was already off to a horrible start. There was no icebreaker. There was no agenda. In this meeting, I was left with more questions than answers, more confusion than certainty and more tears than triumph. You see, this was not just an ordinary meeting. My friends, this meeting was with a teacher called pain.

As I scrambled to put my life back together, cancel wedding venues, pay for a dress I would never use, and face the new normal in my life, I would be asked to several more impromptu meetings with pain. Every week this meeting happened and the pain intensified. Within the next month, I would find that my ex had a sexual addiction which led him to sleep with at least five women while we were engaged. I would attempt to make things work for the sake of the relationship and I introduced him to one of the best counselors I knew but I found that I was losing myself in the process. I asked my Pastor about the plethora of prophecies that my fiancé and I received about our life and ministry, and he told me these life changing words, "God does not change the plan but He will change the man!" I wanted my "normal" back but that was something I knew I could never have.

The final straw was on February 13th, 2015. I was on my way back to my classroom as he had just delivered a teddy bear, a diet coke, and a card to my job. I received a call from a number I had seen before and recognized as his "dispatcher" since he was a truck driver. The voice on the other end was no dispatcher but it was the voice of a prostitute that he hired for sex, caught feelings for, put in an apartment, and paid bills for all while engaged to me. She told me how he would bring her into my home and she described my home to a "T"- from the Ab Lounger in the garage to the Christmas tree in my living room. She told me how she had the Human Papilloma Virus (HPV), described their many encounters, and told me how he stated he was not attracted to me. I told her I had heard enough and exited the phone. The relationship was over but the pain was not.

There were days I would crawl in a ball and cry. I remember being on the phone with my best friend and I was screaming so loudly because I was in so much emotional pain. I would sit and listen to Jessica Reedy's song "Better" over and over again. There were days I thought about suicide and days I just blanked out and didn't know I was in the world. I remember sending my Pastor's wife a text saying, "Please pray for me. I just made it to work and I don't know how I got here!" She and my best friend had to come and get me from work as they did not want me driving. My mind was gone. I couldn't understand why this was happening to me. You see, I did everything right. I was there for him. I prayed for him. Whatever he needed, I became. There was NOTHING he wanted from me that he did not get. This is why when people make the statement saying, "What you won't do another woman will," I simply roll my eyes in disgust because you can do all the right things but if a person is not right, it will all be in vain!

You see, although I was doing everything right by the world's standards, I was not doing everything right by God's standards. I placed my mind, body, and soul in the hands of a man when it should have been placed in the hands of God. I began to ask God how much more pain I could take. I wanted to know how many more meetings I would have. I went to the doctor on April 1st only to find out that I too had HPV- and it was one membrane from becoming cancerous. Within a year from this, I would have at least five procedures and my fertility was almost taken away. There was nothing more I desired than to be a mom and this dream was almost turned into a nightmare due to these reoccurring meetings with a teacher called pain. It's as if the meetings kept coming and the invitations kept piling in and these, my friends, were meetings I could not opt out of. After a few short weeks, I became adjusted to my new normal. The meetings with this teacher called pain seemingly decreased. The tears had stopped. The pain had subsided. I felt all the meetings were finally over and then in the midst of this, on April 11th, 2015 I would suddenly be invited to another meeting only in this meeting I would find that my father suddenly died with no notice.

Many of you, like me, have had a meeting with this teacher called pain. We often sweep the pain under the rug thinking that it will heal itself. We don't deal with the myriad issues that we face and as a result, we neglect to live Happily Single After because pain has made us hard and nonchalant.

Maybe your pain wasn't a pain from a broken relationship like mine was. Maybe your pain is from the molestation by a family member you trusted to protect you. Maybe your pain was from abandonment from your parents. I don't know what your pain is but I can tell you that we all have pain. If we fail to deal with it adequately we will remain victims of scars instead of voices of survivors. I want to share with you a story of a victim of scars from the Bible.

Lessons from Tamar

In 2nd Samuel the 13th chapter we get a glimpse into the life of the children of King David. I encourage you to read 2nd Samuel Chapter 13 to get the entire contextual thought of the principles I will mention below. Here we meet a prince by the name of Amnon. This prince had everything his heart desired- from land to monetary goods- but it was only one thing his heart longed for and that was his sister Tamar. My friends, Tamar didn't know this, but what we will see is that like you and I, Tamar had a meeting with this great teacher called pain. She was invited to help her brother and unbeknownst to her, the help she offered would turn into the pain she would suffer. Before we delve deep into this story I want you to take a moment to read the aforementioned scripture to fully understand what Tamar endured. There are three things we can grasp from Tamar's life to help move us from a meeting with pain to being Happily Single After Pain!

Where does Pain Begin?

Pain begins with an offense from an unclean spirit. If you read 2nd Samuel 13:1-2 you will see that Amnon was so in love with his sister that he couldn't eat and all he could think about was his desire to be with her. Let me put a peg here. Many of us have entered into a painful situation because we, like Amnon, confused love with lust!! I hear you say, "But you don't understand. I love him. He buys me things. He makes me feel good. He takes me out. He's a good looking man." But wait aren't these good things?

1st Corinthians 13:4-7 says:
"Love suffers long *and* is kind; love does not envy; love does not parade itself, is not puffed up; does not behave rudely, does not seek its own, is not provoked, thinks no evil; does not rejoice in iniquity, but rejoices in the truth; bears all things, believes all things, hopes all things, endures all things."

In other words, if it is the opposite of any of these things I submit to you that you are not in love, but you are in lust. Anything you just "gotta have" and can't shake is lust. We have some single people who lust behind the idea of being married. You have your wedding colors picked out and bridesmaids' dresses preordered but there is only one problem. You don't have a groom and you aren't even in a relationship. In order to live Happily Single After you have to stop chasing your lust and go after your love... But I digress.

Ephesians 6:12
"For we wrestle not against flesh and blood but against powers, against rulers of darkness of this world, against spiritual wickedness in high places."

It is not a person that hurt you but it is a spirit within them that caused the hurt. God said this to me during my pain and it totally shook my beliefs. He said, "I love the person who hurt you just as much as I love you!" Let that marinate for a moment. *God loves both the abuser and the victim. He loves both the saint and the sinner.* This is a hard concept to grasp at first because it seems as if we are letting the person who caused us pain off the hook but this is far from the truth. Remember we talked about knowing God as ABBA? When a father loves his children he disciplines them according to what they do. He loves them the same but he will have compassion on the one that is in pain and chastise the one who causes pain. I had to realize that no matter how angry I was that God's repayment was much better than any repayment I could give.

Tamar was King David's daughter and was described as beautiful. She was born of royalty but yet that royalty did not stop her from having a meeting with this teacher called pain. She was deceived, tricked, and raped. We see how she was doing the right thing and doing what her father commanded but at the end of the day she still ended up wounded. A woman who is Happily Single After understands that she is from royalty should never allow pain to remove her from her throne.

Tamar's abuser raped her. He had now gotten the thing he wanted but the Bible declares that now the hate for which he hated her was greater than the love with which he loved her. She did no wrong but now she was hated by the one who did her wrong. Listen, when you know you have done everything right, when you know you have stayed in the will of God, don't allow anyone to tell you that your pain is your fault. I remember people asking me, "Well what did you do to make your ex do what he did?" I even had others ask, "Well what DIDN'T you do to make him cheat?" Shame hit me because I start bargaining. "Well maybe if I did this, then he would've done this." I thought that maybe if I was smaller or prettier then he would have loved me like I loved him. Listen, when someone is overtaken by a spirit, it has nothing to do with what you did or didn't do. Often friends, family, and society victimize the victim. When this happens people try to find a cause and effect as to why you experienced the pain you have endured. Do not allow anyone to tell you that the cause of your pain is your fault! People who are Happily Single After understand that they cannot be victimized for being the victim of pain.

No one gets to dictate how you deal with pain BUT you are responsible for your response to pain. I remember taking all of my ex's items that were in my possession to Goodwill, emptying his bank account, and sending the picture to everyone in his phone as the phone was in my name and I had access to his contacts. This was my REACTION to pain. I wanted him to feel what I felt. People who had never been through the situation began to judge my reaction without empathizing with my pain. In hindsight, I can see the error of my ways but at the moment I was reacting to presented stimuli. *In order to be Happily Single After, you must recognize that pain requires a RESPONSE and not a REACTION.* A response is well thought out and carefully planned with the end result being the restoration of self but a reaction is a gut movement that has little thought and the aim is often revenge. In order to be Happily Single After Pain, we must let go of the need for revenge and embrace the need for restoration!

Why Does Pain Continue?

Pain continues when we forget who we are! 2nd Samuel 13:17-19 said that Tamar tore her robe. Her robe signified royalty. It signified her birthright. She took off the very thing that defined her destiny. Many of us, like Tamar, have allowed pain and hurt to stop us from believing that we are who God says we are and that we will do what God says we will do. *I have come to serve notice on the devil that is speaking to you that you will do all that God has destined for you to do. You will be all who God promised you to be.* Your pain was not a setback. Your pain literally set you up for all God wants to do in your life.

I remember going through my pain and the enemy told me a series of negative phrases such as, "You will never have anyone to love you! You are too fat to be loved. You are too this to have that." In those times I had to speak to the enemy and say, "I am the righteousness of God created in Christ Jesus. I am the head and not the tail- above only and not beneath. I can have ALL that God promised me and if nobody ever loves me, I'm going to love myself!!" *Happy singles make declarations every day that go against the lies the enemy wants them to believe. They meditate on good things and live a life built on positivity. They speak back to those thoughts and say things like, "If nobody ever takes me out, I will take myself out!" They say, "If nobody ever believes in me, I will believe in myself!"* When you are Happily Single After Pain, you know the importance of being comfortable with YOU without allowing pain to rob you of being you.

Pain also continues because often we want others to cater to our pain instead of forcing us to deal with our pain. We become sensitive about the area of our pain so much until it pushes people away from us because we have "protected" that area for so long. We attempt to cover the wound but the smell of the wound seeps through in the form a bad attitude, hyper-aggression, depression, promiscuity, or even inflicting pain on others- knowingly or unknowingly. Covered wounds won't heal but they sure can remain infected! Happy singles understand that they cannot walk around infected by pain and they must uncover pain in order for God to cover your pain. Think about that for a moment. What you choose to cover, God cannot cover or protect! When you surrender that pain, His protection becomes evident. Often while we are dealing with a covered wound we develop the mindset that others have to accept the "smell" of our wound without us ever having to do anything to change it. We want others to "fix" our pain.

I see women all the time mention how they can't wait to have a man that will restore them and heal them. Can I be real with you for a moment? You may find a man to do that for you and that's great! Here's the ugly reality. It is nobody's job to fix the aftermath of your pain but YOU! *Someone may have caused your pain but no one is responsible for the smell that emanates from it but you.* People who are Happily Single After take ownership of the aftermath of their pain. They don't sit around in sorrow and loathing in their pain nor do they make excuses for behaviors associated with their pain. They emerge from it as a butterfly emerges from a cocoon because they know that it is the cocoon that sets the stage for something beautiful to spring forth. In order to be Happily Single After Pain, you must embrace the painful situation and begin to fix yourself instead of waiting for someone else to fix you. You cannot move on to your Happily Ever After as a damaged person. When you are Happily Single After Pain you embrace wholeness because you understand that in order to have a Happily Ever After you have to fix *you* so you won't break the purpose that is assigned for your life.

"Don't allow your pain to take you where your promises never destined you."

Tamar's pain took her from living in a palace to living in what was called a harem. A harem was a separate place in the household where female servants and concubines lived. It was a far cry from the life she was promised. She went from living in the palace to residing in the pit. Don't allow your pain to take you where your promises never destined you. You were designed for the palace so stop living in the pit! Pit living changes your lifestyle from that of a Queen to that of a concubine. It changes your character. You cannot continue to allow pain to change your character. You know that your character is changing because you say things like, "I will never be loyal to another person again!" This comes from a place of pain because you were loyal in your last relationship. Loyalty is who you are! Who are you to allow pain to change that? You say that you will never trust again but trust is embedded in your DNA! *Pain does change us because it teaches us life lessons BUT do not allow pain to stop you from being you!*

Tamar tore her robe which was a symbol of her tearing off her royalty and taking on pit living. I can hear her saying, "God, I had a life that was secure. God, I had a wonderful life planned and now it seems as if the very thing I was born for is the thing I will die without." Every hope and dream she had was dismantled by the acts of another. Some of you have felt this same way. It's as if everything you have gone through has removed the promise from your life. God's promise is a promise. If He said it, it will come to pass. Begin to thank Him because no matter what has happened TO you, God's work will still be done THROUGH you!

When Does Pain End?

Pain ends when you make a decision for it to end. Your invitation to the meeting with pain was not your decision, but you have a decision on when it ends. There are two major decisions you have to make. The first decision you have to make is a decision to forgive. Listen, unforgiveness is like drinking poison and expecting the other person to die. I was watching a show on MTV called "Behind the Music" and it featured the iconic rapper L.L.

Cool J. He said a powerful quote that sticks with me even today. He said, "I forgive all who have hurt me because, at the end of the day, they are just teachers!" What has your pain taught you? *The difference between an egg and a potato that are both placed in hot water is that the water causes the potato to soften and the egg to harden.* Happy singles understand the importance of allowing pain to soften their heart instead of hardening their character. They use pain as a catalyst for growth and not a cause of groaning.

I am an extreme lover of music! One of my favorite songs is by Betty Wright and is called "No Pain, No Gain!" In the song she says these words:

"There was an old lady sitting under a tree, she called me over and she said to me, my days left here may not be long. I wouldn't waste my time telling you nothing wrong. See love is a flower it needs the sun and the rain, a little bit of pleasure worth a whole lot of pain. If you learn this secret- how to forgive, a longer and a better life you'll live! NO Pain!! NO GAIN!!"

What have you gained from your pain? People who are Happily Single After Pain understand that with NO PAIN, there can be NO GAIN!

After you have made the decision to forgive you now have to make a decision to move forward. *Many of us are missing our Happily Ever After because the pain of our past has blinded us to the promise of our future. You cannot move forward looking in the rearview mirror!*

Tamar's name meant Palm Tree. If you know anything about the palm tree, you know that a palm tree can withstand hurricane force winds. Because it is so grounded, a palm tree will bend but it will not break. Many of you have been like the palm tree. What was meant to break you only bent you. What was meant to uproot you only grounded you. What was meant to destroy you ultimately destined you. Happy singles understand the importance of bending without breaking. Don't allow what was meant to bend you to break you.

Tamar put ashes on her head. Ashes were a sign of mourning. The Bible says that weeping may endure for a night but joy comes in the morning. The difference between your mourning season and your morning is you!! You make or break pain off of your life. It's time for you to make a decision. Do you arise and put your robe back on and remove the ashes of mourning from your head and begin to live a life of Happily Single After Pain, or do you choose to sit in your pain and allow pain to distract you from receiving your Happily Ever After? You cannot be Happily Single After while holding on to pain. Today you have to let it go!

Your pain HAD to happen. There is a purpose behind everything. I didn't understand the purpose of my pain when all of this was going on. I was so broken. I still have certain triggers that can take me back to the pain I felt that day such as Jessica Reedy's song. Just because you have triggers does not mean you are still holding on to it. Often, we hear the words forgive and forget. It is not humanly possible to forgive and forget. How can you forget what has pained you? I would say that to be Happily Single After Pain you must FORGIVE and move FORWARD. We don't hold the offense against the person and we work on being whole. You being Happily Single After will demand that you become whole while you wait on your Happily Ever After. It is this wholeness that will produce lasting results for generations to come and enhance the overall complexion of your life. You may ask how I became whole after my pain. I talked about it with others and this liberated me. I didn't act like I was fine when I wasn't. Then I began to work on me. You can be Happily Single After Pain- and I am a living witness!

Let Me Pray For You!

God I come thanking you for the person who is reading this right now. You know their point of pain. You know the thing that has caused them to toil at night. Lord, someone is dealing with the pain of abuse as a child while another is dealing with the pain of a divorce. I ask that you show them your love in the midst of pain. We thank you that we will walk Happily Single After Pain. We will not allow pain to harden us but to make us soft in our hearts so we can love harder and live harder. We thank you for healing us from it all now!

In Jesus' Name!

Amen!

Chapter Five

Happily Single After Dating Dilemmas

ating dilemmas. Haven't we all had them? The face of dating has changed abundantly over the past twenty years. Think about the days when a guy would nervously ask a woman out on a date. When she agreed, he pulled up to her home dressed as sharp as can be and brought with him a single rose as a sign of generosity. As she walks out of the house, he ensures that she is safe by opening the car door for her and cautiously closing it after she is completely secured in the car. She is now blushing because she is enamored by him being such a gentleman. They pull up to a nice restaurant that unbeknownst to her, he had been saving for some time to take her. He pulls out her chair and pushes it back in as she sits. Then they share a laugh or two and talk about future plans. The check comes and it is no question of who would pay the bill as he reaches for his wallet with no hesitation. He then walks his lady to the car and drives her back home all while anticipating the first kiss. As they pull up to the house, he nervously walks her to the door and- with her permission- kisses her softly and slowly walks back to his car as she stands at the door and watches him walk away. They have already made plans to speak the next day and instantly they knew that they had found "the one." There is only one problem. This is so 1900's!!

If the truth were to be told, we now live in what is called a hook-up culture. Sex before a relationship is the norm and it often leaves both parties questioning the authenticity of real love. We meet, have sex, and then attempt to get to know one another- all in the quest to find our Happily Ever After. This is normally not the outcome as pain comes and the single parties are now searching for the next person that can be interviewed for this uninhabited position. I will talk about sex extensively in the next chapter but sex often leads to dating dilemmas that hinder our ability to be Happily Single After.

Technology

Recently I wanted to look for a new pair of shoes. I absolutely HATE shopping! My only hope was to go on the internet and look for the perfect pair. I searched and I searched until I found the shoes that were pleasing to my eye. There were multiple shoes in my cart however, in the end, the search was narrowed to one pair. This is how dating has turned in modern years. Online dating is now a thing, whether we like it or not. Antiquated dating advice tells the single person to avoid online dating at all cost. This is not a modern day reality. Often those who have been married for a decade or more don't understand the new challenges in being single and this includes the idea of using technology to find a mate.

In the modern world of dating, traditional courtship is a thing of the past. Technology is often the instrument for which individuals utilize in an effort to meet one another. Our dating may go a little more like the following scenario. Guy sees a picture of a girl that he likes on Facebook. Guy then sends the girl a message with the words, "Hey beautiful!" The girl responds with a simple, "Hi!" A conversation would then commence and the male now asks the female for her number. She graciously complies and a phone conversation ensues. Then they agree to "meet-up" at a local coffee shop to have their first official meeting. If they like what they see and hear, more phone conversations ensue and then the uncertainty of a relationship becomes a common theme. Texting is the norm between them and face to face communication is minimal if at all. Both parties have more "internet interests" as often neither party is invested into forming a committed monogamous relationship.

There are cautions in dating online but these are the same precautions that any sane human being should take even when meeting face to face. Several years ago I remember meeting a guy online. He was suave and smooth and claimed that his name was Diego. He seemed accomplished and stated that he had no kids and a budding business. This guy was outwardly a good catch. He gave this long spill about how he wanted to marry me and meet my family- all after the first meeting. Sometimes we as Christian women are so naive and we think that if it's fast then it must be God. I would say this is often the opposite. After my first meeting with this man, I begin to do research based on the information he provided to me. I found out that his name was not Diego. He was not ex-military as he claimed and he had gone around the country as a con artist swindling women out of thousands of dollars and often leaving them with children that he did not support. The news station even did a story about him and his evil ways. I was so grateful that I dodged a major bullet. Many would use this story as a reason to not date online, however I have met people in person who were just a crazy as the aforementioned man. *A person who is Happily Single After Dating Dilemmas understands that the mate of our choice may not come through traditional means but we must be open and use discernment with any individual that we meet.*

If you choose to use online dating as a tool, research the person extensively. You can perform Google searches of the person and use your local police department to check criminal records. There are resources available to help you stay safe and to help you avoid being "catfished." Check to make sure the individual has an active presence on social media. If they don't this is an automatic red flag. You may be thinking, "Well some people don't do social media." This is true but if you use an online dating service to find them then I would be willing to bet that they have an online social media presence. Checking things upfront can help you to avoid being Happily Miserable After your next internet quest.

Dating has changed but the necessity for companionship has not changed. Gender roles have shifted as often women are in a greater position to have earning power that is above that of her male counterparts. Nowadays men do not need a woman to cook and clean because often their mothers have taught them how to be self-sufficient as these same mothers have seen a major shift in traditional gender roles and want to prepare their sons for this shift. Household responsibilities are often shared as the working woman and working man collaborate to make life happen. Women are less impressed by a man that wants to run her bath water and romanticize them and they are more impressed by a man who can relieve the pressure of her day to day life such as helping with a common interest or showing her that he has the capacity to provide for her the things that she cannot provide for herself. Many men and women are delaying courtship because they have found a lack of suitable companionship as the attributes of men and women have changed significantly.

A Dying Breed of Men

Growing up my example of manhood came from my father. He was suave, smooth and without a doubt he was the head of our household. What he said is what happened. My dad was what many would consider to be an Alpha Male. The Alpha Male concept is one in which men were manly men that brought home the bacon and were the leaders of their households. They took care of home financially but often offered little emotional support. Alpha men are seen as the leader of the pack, and the one who provides and protects. They are not attention seekers but they are go-getters. When we look on social media and even turn on the television, this is not the genre of men that we see. This, my friends, is a dying breed.

Ladies, the Alpha Male that you are seeking to lead you may not be a reality. Some (not all) men today are often comfortable with not having to be the breadwinners and many are comfortable with a mediocre life. When dating, you have to make a decision as to whether you will wait to find that man that exhibits Alpha Male tendencies or if you will be just as happy with dealing with a Beta Male. The Beta Male is the man who is often indecisive because he makes very careful decisions and the joy factor has often left because his decision making can be slow. He puts other people before himself and may seem like a servant type. He is the one who will cook for you and clean but he will run from commitment. Beta men may not be assertive so it may be hard to understand what they want from the relationship. Because of this, we as women have to have the dreaded "DTR" conversation that I will talk about shortly.

We are not living in an age where most men are assertive about their wants and desires as far as relationships are concerned. This is the cause for women stepping up and being very aggressive.

Alpha men are turned off by this type of woman. They prefer a woman that allows them to do the pursuing and won't take an aggressive stance towards a relationship. Remember, he is a natural leader and wants to feel as if he has claimed his prize by pursuing you. A woman who is Happily Single After has no problems with being patient and allowing the man to pursue. She knows that she must maintain her status and stance as a lady because if not, she will be seen as a part of the next group of women.

A Dying Breed of Women

Now sisters, you didn't think that I would let you off the hook, did you? Remember the days of Big Mama? Remember how you could depend on her wisdom and be secure in her care? Big Mama was the neighborhood mom that we can always count on for our meals, tears, and prayers. She knew how to maintain her family and survive off of nothing if that meant her kids would have something. She went to work, came home to cook and still had time to ensure the needs of her kids were met. Big Mama had a soft strength where she can be firm with the kids but soft and loving toward her man. Her man never felt disrespected but he felt supported and affirmed. Sadly, the generation of Big Mama has died.

Women have lost the "softness" that is characteristic of classical womanhood. Life has made us so hard. A short while ago I was in one of my social media groups and a question was posed. The question said, "Why are so many strong black women still single?" I pondered this question for quite some time. I then responded in the following manner:

"We have been so hurt and damaged by the wrong man that we build up walls. What we don't realize is that subconsciously we become the very thing that has hurt us. We become so strong to the point of "manliness." When a man sees us, he has to see something that he is missing. When Eve was presented to Adam he saw what he was missing. He did not see another man but he saw a WO-man or WOMB-man created from him and for him. But now we as women have allowed pain to make us hard and we have negated the WOMB-man by simply becoming like men. Men are not seeing their missing piece. This is why I get nervous when I hear a woman say, "I act like a man!" Acting like a man is never who she was called to be but this mentality comes from a place of pain and self-sufficiency. We will still be single until he finds something in us that is missing from the depths of him."

Softness. This is a part of the dying breed of women in the world today. Society looks upon women as if it is weak to be "soft." However, when I speak of softness I mean softness in your character, appearance and your emotions. Many single women are so combative and feisty until this scares potential suitors away. We carry a hard attitude and harsh demeanor. This is not who we were created to be. Softness does not mean that you are a passive doormat without an opinion. It means that you have the power to respectfully speak your opinion and not harbor feelings of anger or pride. It actually is a sign of your strength. This is why finding the right man who can allow you to be soft is critical to your womanhood. *A weak and passive man will always make you feel the need to be hard. It takes a strong woman to act in a way opposite to society. It takes a strong woman to admit that there is nothing wrong with classical womanhood.* You can be a woman and soft at the same time.

I can recall at one point I was extremely hard. I felt as if I had to be that way so no one would mess with me. As a result, no one would *mess* with me- not even potential suitors. I prayed and did an all liquid fast for three days because I didn't want to be hard. I wanted to be soft and loving. I knew that hard women won't let anyone in and this causes even more dating dilemmas. I was not Happily

Single After until I allowed God to prick my heart and remove the pain of dating dilemmas and make me soft again. A woman who is Happily Single After understands the importance of being "soft" and knows that softness does not make you weak but in turn you become stronger.

We have turned away from the soft woman and warped into the Alpha Female. The Alpha Female is seen as dominant and domineering. She is career focused and can do what she wants when she wants to. While there is absolutely nothing wrong with being an Alpha Female often this woman does not know how to take leadership from a male and this may cause her Happily Ever After to end in Miserably Divorced After! I can identify with this woman because she is like me in so many ways. I have been on my own since I was 18 years old and have lived alone since I graduated college. It is hard for me to fathom giving up my independence to a man. But, I, like every other single woman, must learn that in order to be Happily Single After I must embrace the reality of interdependence as I approach my Happily Ever After. Men want to feel needed and often the Alpha Female feels she can do it all on her own and she isn't afraid to tell you this. She must learn to balance softness with the need to be dominant in every situation in order to live Happily Single After.

Why Good Girls Like Bad Boys

I will be the first to admit this. I am a good girl that likes bad boys. It's something about their cockiness and aggressiveness that is highly attractive. This, unfortunately, has caused me a lot of hurt and pain. One attraction that drives good girls to like bad boys is the fact that bad boys are often closely aligned with the Alpha Male. Now, Alpha Men are not necessarily bad boys, but bad boys carry the desirable characteristics of an Alpha Male. The stereotypical bad boy is one that knows what he wants. When he approaches a woman he does it with no hesitation and often his confidence is through the roof. He is a protector and she feels safe around him. He walks with swagger and talks with charm. This charm causes a play on the emotions of a good girl. *The way to a woman's heart is through her ears.* He knows how to say, what to say, and is calculated on when to say it. By the time she realizes it, a dating dilemma has now unfolded. He has gotten to her heart through her ears and now she is so deep that she is at a point of no return.

The good girl will stay in this relationship with the bad boy because she is good and what do good people do? They aim to fix people. She makes excuses for his behavior such as, "He is so busy with work so he doesn't have time for me and that's ok." She might even say, "He hit me because he was stressed out. He didn't mean it and that's ok." This is not ok! He now becomes her focus because she is busy trying to fix that which is broken. She throws all caution to the wind because she is still hooked on the unfulfilled words that have been spoken to her by the bad boy. He apologizes and she takes him back and unfortunately the cycle continues until she is empty and depleted of her very being. She has lost herself trying to help him find himself. This, my friends, is a dangerous zone. The woman who is Happily Single After knows how to back away after she sees the initial signs of disaster in this bad boy such as excuses, missed dates, and inconsistencies.

Here's another reason women like me are erroneously fond of bad boys. We have never seen an example of true love from a man so we seek it in the bad boy. A bad boy won't begin to show you his true colors until he has convinced you that he loves you. The good girl thinks that it is real because she doesn't know that real love never hurts. This is the type of man chosen by her mother and siblings so surely this is the type of man that she should date. Many times her father was not around to show her an example. Before she realizes it she is on a path to temptation and because she hasn't seen an example she thinks the good boy is lame therefore she passes him up or friend-zones him. Nice guys will finish last because they are non-assertive and their overall intent is often not known. She doesn't realize that good men still exist but they often don't come in the package she expects. She's now in her late 20's, has never been loved, and has settled for life being the way that she currently sees it. A woman who is Happily Single After understands that just because she has never seen an example of a good man doesn't mean that she has to settle for a bad boy.

The Church and Dating

Most of the dating advice Christians receive comes from the church. We, as the church, have offered antiquated dating advice based on how the world was and not for our modern reality. This is one problem I have with the church as we know it and their approach to singles. The Alpha Male is seen as the prize and the Alpha Female is seen as the problem. We teach singles how to prepare for marriage but we neglect to teach them how to be successful singles. We push single women into pre-marital courses but we rarely push them into entrepreneurial courses. As a result, single women in the church have been taught to cater fully to a man that may never exist. Men are often pacified for their behavior and not held to the same relational standards as women. The church and our views will keep you single and unhappy. Why? Because when we are constantly developing a single person towards marriage and not towards being a complete single discouragement transpires. The focus becomes marriage and when marriage does not happen the person is ruined and disappointed.

There are two scriptures that are commonly used by the church as related to singles and their development. The first scripture we want to look at is Proverbs 18:22 (NKJV):

"He who finds a wife finds a good thing and obtains favor from the Lord."

Think about how this is often conveyed to singles in the church. To the single woman it is said, "You shouldn't be looking for a man anyway. He should find you!" This may mess up some of your theologies but this scripture has nothing to do with a single woman and how her quest for companionship should be. During the time of the Bible marriages, were arranged and we are not living in that day. To be scripturally accurate we need to understand the root of the scripture. The word "find" in this scripture is from the Hebrew word "matsa." This word means to acquire or to get.

Basically, this means that the man who "gets" or obtains a wife gets a good thing and obtains favor with God. What this does not mean is that a woman has to sit idly and wait for a man to approach her or "choose" her. My college roommate is now happily married but she approached her husband first and he then did the pursuing. It is perfectly ok to approach a man but this approach should never be a chase as it is still his job to pursue.

Due to the being "found" mentality, women often sit around saying, "Why won't someone ever choose me!" No ma'am. You have a choice in who you are to be in a relationship with as well. It is a mutual decision and not some "choice" that is solely the responsibility of another to make. This is why men can be perpetrators of pain to women in the church and also why women settle for the first man that approaches them. We think because he has "found" us in the church then he is the one. This can be the furthest thing from the truth. You have to realize that this scripture is actually saying "He who GETS a wife." There are implications to this for the man who "GETS" a wife. The implication is that he finds favor. **You are a man's favor!** Let's take a second to think back to the Garden of Eden. Adam was NEVER looking for a wife and Eve was not looking to be "found." Let that sink in. Adam IDENTIFIED his wife. How did he identify her? She had something that he was missing which was his rib (remember we talked about the other slipper). He was the one resting in his singleness and she was presented to him. He did not find Eve. She was presented to him. *Both the single male and female must rest in their singleness and allow God to do the presenting.*

This is why you should never have to have the dreaded "DTR" (Define the Relationship) conversation with any person. Defining the relationship is a mutual choice and not a one person decides all event. As a hint, most of the time when you have to have the DTR conversation, the relationship is headed nowhere because when two people genuinely want each other then intentions are made known. I was dating this guy who stated that he had a strong interest in me. He pursued me abundantly, and we hit it off perfectly. He would not define the relationship or commit. I did everything in my power to try to make it work. Nothing worked. He eventually ended up dating his ex. He gave signs of non-commitment but I wanted him to "choose" me. Instead, he chose her. I should have made the decision to leave at the point of non-commitment but I was blinded by the concept of being "found." A woman who is Happily Single After understands that she is the "prize" and the favor and because of this she can be confident in her dating life and decisions thereof.

This scripture also has implications for men. Remember we spoke about how the Alpha Male is a dying breed? Alpha Men are pursuers. Many men are not pursuers these days. Pressure has been placed on Beta Men who do not display Alpha Men qualities to be in constant pursuit of finding that perfect woman. He may be turned away from the woman that approaches him because he, too, has been taught that it is his job to pursue. *There is a difference between pursuing and approaching. Approaching shows interest but pursuing shows intent.* Men do not have to do the approaching to be the pursuers.

Let's look at one more scripture. I believe this scripture defines what we should really do in our time of singleness. Let's take a look at 1st Corinthians 7:32-35 (MSG):

"I want you to live as free of complications as possible. *When you're unmarried, you're free to concentrate on simply pleasing the Master.* Marriage involves you in all the nuts and bolts of domestic life and in wanting to please your spouse, leading to so many more demands on your attention. The time and energy that married people spend on caring for and nurturing each

other, *the unmarried can spend in becoming whole and holy instruments of God.* I'm trying to be helpful and make it as easy as possible for you, not make things harder. All I want is for you to be able to develop a way of life in which you can spend plenty of time together with the Master without a lot of distractions."

This is one of the few scriptures in the Bible that outlines where we should be as singles. Our focus should be on becoming whole as singles. The myth that marriage completes us is a lie. There is a difference between being healed and being whole. *You are healed if you no longer suffer from an ailment or offense. You are whole when that offense or ailment no longer suffers because of you.* Wholeness is only when we can move past the things that have caused us to be uneasy and look at them as a moment and not a monument. It was something that came to pass but it isn't something that came to stay. Healing is being free from it but wholeness is when you come in oneness within yourself. We should be Happily Single After before we obtain our Happily Ever After. Our focus should not be on the marriage but on being the best us we can be in spirit, soul, and body. Focusing on marriage instead of preparing yourself to be Happily Single After will always leave you disappointed and frustrated. As a happy single you must focus on

YOU in this season and be the total package for the life you have NOW!

The Coming to America Mentality

Remember the 1980's cult classic movie *Coming to America*? I'm sure you could probably recite several lines from the movie right now. Many of us have what I like to call the "Coming to America Mentality" when it comes to dating. Think about the scene when the woman who was chosen to become Hakeem's wife was introduced to him. He took her in the chambers to meet with her privately. Then he asks her a series of questions. "What kind of music do you like?" She says, "Whatever kind of music you like." He says, "Do you have a favorite food?" She responded, "Whatever kind of food you like." All of her life she had been trained to be married to the Prince. She did not know who she was because she was so busy trying to learn who he was. She had no idea of her identity or what she liked. This, my friends, is the Coming to America Mentality.

On my quest for Happily Single After I began this concept that I created called "The 50 Date Challenge." I challenged myself to take myself on 50 dates alone in a year. These dates were to be to events that I normally would not have attended such as plays, concerts, and even solo trips. I wanted to find out what I liked so that when I met a man I would not be like the woman in *Coming to America*. I dated myself. This means I spent time alone learning me. I learned areas of my life that needed to change but I also learned that there were parts of me that I absolutely loved. A person who is Happily Single After Dating Dilemmas understands that sometimes it is best to take a break from the dating scene to learn who they are and what they like. They understand that when they are confident in themselves, it will draw confident people to their lives.

Dating yourself is one of the most powerful and effective tools you can use as a single person. It's a time for freedom to explore you. During this time you expose yourself to another way of life. Have you really taken the time to learn who you are and what you like or will your response be, "Whatever you like?" Have you taken time to travel or learn a new skill? Do you know what you really like? When a man approaches you, your likes should include more than attending church, choir rehearsal, or even your job. It's time to let go of the Coming to America Mentality and embrace the fact that you have a mind and a choice in life. You cannot be Happily Single After without knowing your identity and purpose for living.

When to Date You

One mistake I made in dating was jumping from relationship to relationship without first dealing with the residue from the previous relationship. Please stop jumping from one person to the next! Jumping from relationship to relationship is like dipping yourself in red paint. You never wash this off so now you dip yourself in blue paint to cover the red paint. You never wash this off so now you dip in yellow paint. The stain from the other paint is still there hidden under each layer and we never wash it off in hopes that one coat of paint would cover the other coat. Get the picture? You now carry the residue from one relationship to the next and you have never properly dealt with the issues from any of them. The root of all of this is loneliness. A person who is Happily Single After dating dilemmas understands that loneliness is not an option. They know how to remain single until they find the one with their other slipper.

There are many times in your life when it is best to date you and only you. You should not date another person if you are fresh out of a relationship. We dress this up on the outside like we are fine but we are not. We hear that the best way to get over your ex is to move to your next. That temporary rebound will not erase the years of pain you have endured from the last relationship. A person who is Happily Single After understands the importance of taking a break and getting you together before trying to get together with another person. You should also not date if you need time to grow personally. This could mean self-improvements and self-building. This process is often time-consuming and it will change you. You do not need any distractions on your way to a better you. The next time in your life that you should date you and you alone is when you are not stable in life. If you are in between jobs or even mentally unstable then dating someone else should not be an option. I recently had a conversation with a gentleman that wanted to date me. He is very nice and loved Jesus but he was financially unstable. My words to him were, "Please, do not attempt to pursue me if you are not ready for marriage in all areas!" His financial situation was dire and I knew this would cause strife in the relationship before it even began. This brings me to my last point. You should not date if you are not ready for commitment. You are playing with the heart and emotions of another individual. If you are not 100% ready then do not risk hurting another person for the sake of temporary pleasure. A person who is Happily Single After understands that it is better to take care of oneself than to risk another person's heartbreak.

Dating Differently

Insanity is defined as doing the same things over and over expecting different results. After I went through the pain of ruptured relationships I realized one fact. In order to get what I never had, I had to do what I had never done. I realized that all of my intimate relationships ended with hurt and pain caused by another. What was the common denominator in all these relationships? I was! It was time for me to date differently. I could no longer date the same way. I tried dating diverse types of men but the way I dated was still based on my prior experiences and I had to do things another way.

The first step that I had to take was to become the person that I wanted to attract. After my break up, I felt unattractive and my self-esteem was at an all-time low. I had to take back my life one step at a time. This is when I began to seek counseling. I also worked with a relationship coach, David Burrus, to help me realize why I was making the same mistakes in relationships over and over again. I will tell you a little about this later. Now that I was working on my mind I knew that I had to work on my body as well. I was overweight and hated the person I had been looking at in the mirror. Some people can be overweight and happy but that's not my testimony. I was at the point that I would rather die than to continue to live in the body I had. I took a huge risk and went to Mexico and underwent a gastric sleeve surgery which reduced the amount of food I could consume. Yes, this was drastic and no it was not the easy way out. I realized that I had been using food as a crutch to deal with emotional pain and I could not be a Happily Single After woman with any addictions holding me hostage. A person who is Happily Single After understands that self-improvement is the key to being consistently happy.

I wanted to attract something better so I became someone better- mentally, physically, spiritually, and emotionally. I became whole. What you are is what you attract. Why do you keep attracting men that aren't whole? It's because you are not whole. Magic transpires when two whole people connect and make purpose happen together. *We don't realize it but who we attract is a reflection of who we are.* We place a value upon ourselves and people will only buy at the price we are selling. We allow people to treat us like pennies when we are really two dollar bills- rare and uncommon. As I increased my value, so did those around me. It will be the same with you. Stop selling yourself for less than your value! When you understand your worth you will stop giving people discounts.

A Better Way to Date

I was out with one of my friends and she met a guy. He wasn't that great looking but he had a smooth foreign accent and charismatic character. Immediately this friend began to plan her life with him and exclaim how much she liked him- all after meeting him and hanging with him for an hour. This wasn't just her case but this is the case for many of us when we meet a man. We have the tendency of planning a life with a man as soon as we meet him. Before he shows mutual interest we have planned our next date, marriage and how many children we will have- all before accessing the character of the individual. When he doesn't meet our expectations, we become disappointed. *You see, most women date off feelings when we should date off standards!* One of the things I worked with my relationship coach on was developing a set of standards and core values that each man that entered my life had to display. These standards help me to decide what man best fits my needs and purpose. If a man doesn't meet these eight core values, then I automatically know that he is not the one and I do not entertain him further. My standards include loyalty, a commitment to abstinence and several other values. When in doubt, I always go back to my standards.

We have not learned how to date as single people. We have the mentality that we should date first and pray and ask God if they are the one second. This is an error-filled mindset that only leads to destruction. *Prayer should happen in ALL stages of dating- especially in the beginning when people are putting their best foot forward. They wear the cologne of their personalities but we often don't see their character- how they really smell until much later.* There are so many theories on dating so it can be a daunting task to ascertain who you should date. I want to share with you how my dating life has evolved and the stages of a relationship with the boundaries of each. If you date according to these stages, you can eliminate many hours of heartache, pain and wasted time.

Stage One- Friendship

This is the stage where you are getting to know a person for who they are. You are testing their loyalty and commitment. It's the stage that you will build with any person that is coming into your life, be it for romantic or platonic purposes. This includes talking on the phone and hanging out in public but only occasionally. This stage is NOT exclusive. A problem we make in the relationship stages is that we rush from friendship to courtship and this should NEVER happen. There are boundaries to this level. There are no expectations in this stage. We do not rush because we understand the importance of building a foundation and knowing this person before we make an exclusive commitment.

We want relationship privileges at the friendship level and this should never be. Be careful of this. There is no sex involved. You do not spend private time alone together. You do not lock them down in this stage or offer relationship benefits such as cooking, cleaning, or any activity to attempt to "prove" to them that you are a good fit for their life. You are simply engaging in communication. During this stage, you do not ask questions such as, "I haven't heard from you in a while." You simply let things fall as they may. The purpose is to get to know a person's character. This stage could last a month or a lifetime. I would suggest at least three months so that you can have time to see what changes they make in that 90 days. Always pray to find out a person's purpose in your life.

Stage Two-Dating

Dating is the second stage and is also non-exclusive. I am a strong advocate of dating multiple people simultaneously. WHAT? Yes! I believe that we should date multiple people in order to keep our options open, keep us focused on our standards and goals, and to find the right fit for our lives. We have a tendency of committing to one person too fast and too soon. The only way dating multiple people works is with a commitment to abstinence and strong boundaries. I will talk about the abstinence commitment more in the next chapter.

In the dating stage, you will hang out more regularly with the person. The purpose of this is to test their suitability to be a mate. You are still not having sex with this person as you are not looking to have a sexual soul tie. Your purpose is to simply get to know the other person on a deeper level. This stage can go down a level to simply friendship or it can move up to courtship. This stage qualifies a person to be exclusive in your life. You are still meeting in public. There are still no relationship privileges or expectations in this stage but this is the decision-making stage.

Think back to when we talked about how entering into a relationship is a mutual decision between two people. You are not only making a choice for you but you are choosing a parent for your future children or step-parent for your current children. A female eagle is very wise in her mate selection. She tests several male eagles during this stage and she is NOT mating with them until she knows that they are a good fit for her life because eagles don't just mate to mate. Eagles mate for life. What she will do is test multiple male eagles by grabbing a small stick and flying high to drop it. If the male eagle can catch it before it hits the ground then she gets a bigger stick to see if he can handle its weight before it hits the ground. She does this to multiple male eagles and if one cannot catch the stick, she drops him from her life. She continues testing the male eagles to see which one can carry the biggest stick. She does this because she knows that if he can catch the biggest stick then he can support and carry her children. The male who does the job more efficiently is the one she chooses to mate with for life. This is how we need to be in the dating stage. We are throwing our "sticks" and ascertaining if the male we are involved with is suitable to carry all of our sticks in life. If not, he can be a good friend but he cannot move into the next stage which is courtship. A person who is Happily Single After understands the importance of not just dating to date but dating with an end goal in mind. They know that settling is not an option and weeding out the weak can make room for the strong.

Stage Three- Courtship

We have confused courtship and dating. This is because we have the rush mentality and often go straight from friendship to courtship. Courtship happens after we have been friends and after we have dated. You have thrown your biggest stick and you know that this is the person who can carry the stick. The purpose of courtship is to ascertain whether or not a person is suitable for marriage. This is an EXCLUSIVE stage where you have weeded out all the other people and you want to focus on one person because they meet your standards and have proven this over time. Again, I will not give you a time on how long this stage should last because this takes prayer and discernment on your part.

During a courtship, you are still not having sex with a person. You can increase your time alone but with grave caution. Many believe that in the courtship stage there is group dating and no affection. You have to know what you can handle. It is not about how close you can get to the stove without being burned. It is about living a life of purpose without trying to test the waters. Group dating isn't always efficient, especially if you are a career person with limited interaction with others and limited time.

This is when you begin to get intimate with the other person. We have been conditioned to think that intimacy and sex are the same things. They are not. Intimacy is INTO-ME-SEE. You are allowing the other person to see into you and the private parts of you. You are seeing if they are everything that you need and if they truly have the other slipper. You are officially in a relationship and you have the freedom of doing more for and with this person. The goal is to continue to build upon a solid foundation of friendship. This again is not a permanent stage. If you cannot deal with some of the intimate details of that person then it is perfectly fine to end the courtship. The purpose of a courtship is to move towards engagement. If it does not, you have made an awesome friend and you have not compromised your body or lifestyle in any way.

Stage Four- Engagement

This is the stage where things are real and you both feel as if you have each other's missing slipper. You have a common purpose and you are striving to reach that common purpose daily. You've decided that the other person has been tested and true and is a potential life partner. You are still not sexually active. You are almost to goal! Wedding dates are set and plans are being made. You are still in prayer and using discernment. Pre-marital counseling should happen during this stage to aid in your discernment. Just because wedding plans are being made does not mean that this stage is permanent, however, if you have built that solid foundation you will now proceed to the last stage that ends your Happily Single After and that is your Happily Ever After!

Stage Five- Marriage

Now that your courtship is over you are now into your Happily Ever After! Marriage! This stage ends your Happily Single After and begins your new life with your new partner. Your focus is now on maximizing your Happily Ever After and building a house on the foundation that has already been laid.

Are these stages foolproof? Of course not! One thing I am sure of is that by following these steps and maintaining the boundaries in each you can truly be Happily Single After and your focus will remain intact. *Remember, we are not dating off of emotions but we are dating with standards and the overall intent is to end in marriage.* A person who is Happily Single After understands the importance of building a firm foundation to avoid the dating dilemmas of the past. Then and only then can we move from our Happily Single After to our Happily Ever After.

Let Me Pray For You!

God I pray for my friend that is reading this right now. I ask that you heal him or her from any dating dilemma that has been presented. Let them know that they can overcome negative mindsets and emotions and that they can live in the abundant life as a single that is dating. Help us to not rush but to use discernment every step of the way. God I pray that they would have destiny partners assigned to their lives and purpose at the appropriate time. No longer shall we have dating dilemmas but we shall have drama-free dating. Although dating has changed, our need for companionship has not and we acknowledge this. Thank you for preparing us for our Happily Ever After!

In Jesus' Name!

Amen!

Chapter Six

Happily Single After Sexual Mishaps

What's a single's book without explicitly talking about the subject of sex? Yes, I am a single Christian and I just said the dirty word SEX!! This is one of the toughest areas to conquer in the single life. I have written to you about some of my struggles in this area and I want to use this chapter to give you a solid plan on how to avoid sexual temptation and live a life free from the attachments caused by sex. The truth is that most of us have done it but not many of us have conquered it.

The struggle lies within the way(s) of the world versus the way of God. Now, if you are looking for a book to tell you that you are going to hell because of sex or condemn you for your past choices, this is certainly not that book. I will not tell you how you will be judged by God but God has consequences for what we do and we are well aware of them.

Bearing in mind that none of us are above reproach, I will extend you the security in knowing that *if in fact you are looking for some solid instructions on how you can be single, saved, and live an abstinent life, I can give you that.* The world has taught us to release and openly display our sexuality. God says to keep our sexuality until we are married. If we are honest, it's hard to live a life of sexual purity- but it is achievable.

When I was about 20 years old I was having a conversation with my youth pastor who had been married for several years. I was so "deep" that I did not face reality about sex. There was a youth who asked about sex and I immediately said with no hesitation, "Sex does not feel good!" This was my jerk reaction because this is what I thought I should say in the church. The youth pastor looked at me with a look of agony and said "Shooooot!! YES IT DOES!" My problem, as is the problem with many singles, was that I was not taught how to balance my sex life in a healthy way. I thought denial of it was the best choice and this is the furthest from the truth.

Sex is great and feels great. What? You are a single Christian and you just said that? YES I DID! Here is the truth. God made sex. God made sex good. But God made sex for married people. We cannot deny the fact that we are sexual beings. *We should actually embrace this. Embracing it does not mean we are practicing it outside of the constraints of marriage. It means that you acknowledge the desire while understanding that there is a proper time to act upon the desire.*

You will either master the area of sex or sex will master you! As I told you before sex was my "fix" when I was going through. After each encounter, I was left with an emptiness like none other. Due to this emptiness, I actually began taking on masculine characteristics. I became the very thing that I felt hurt me. I began to treat sex like men do-and I could literally have a different man each day of the week with no remorse if I chose to. This was not my design as a woman. This was not how I was created to live. I was headed down a path of destruction and I knew that in order for me to get something different, I had to move about my path...well...differently.

That something different was abstinence. *I chose this because I was tired of displeasing God. I was tired of being empty and only getting a temporary fix from the men I encountered. I wanted to know that a man could love me for me and not because of my sexual prowess.* In essence, as the old adage would have it, to get what I never had, I had to do what I had never done. I had attempted abstinence before-often going four years or more then I would fall. The beauty is that God looks at our heart and blots out our repented mistakes. My pastor began teaching on "The Father Daughter Talk" and wrote a book by the same name. A chapter that stuck out in my brain carried the title, "Never lay down your body for a man who has not laid his life down for you!" I realized that I had been laying down my body with those who could not even commit to a relationship with me and this was a problem. Months after making a decision towards abstinence, I read the book "The Wait" by Devon Franklin and Megan Good. This book allowed me to see that I was moving in the right direction. Surely, if these people could wait, so can I. And if I can wait- so can you.

I used to think that the way to a man's heart is through sex. Man, was I wrong! Men just aren't wired to experience sex the way that we do. Many women think that they can sex a man into a relationship so they use sex to bait him. The problem then becomes that she begins to be attached and long for him while in his brain sex is just sex. A man can get sex from anywhere and your sex- as good as you think it is- is no different than what Suzy has to offer. You can give your all to a man and if he is not the right one, no matter how you've sexed him, it still won't work. Since I have been practicing abstinence, men have literally craved being in my presence. I get more from the opposite sex by abstaining than I did when I wasn't. The world teaches us to be sexually free and give sex away as we please. They say that this is control. What I have learned is that I am in more control of my life and dating because I have made a decision towards abstinence.

Listen, you cannot make a decision in the way of abstaining if you do not know your significance, your merit, or your worth. I tell every man I meet from the very first conversation that I am abstinent. Does this run people away? YES, and I could not be more ecstatic! One day I was conversing with a guy and I told him upfront that I was abstinent until marriage. He said, "You lost me at that abstinence stuff!" My response was, "Oh no, you lost *ME* when you said you weren't because I am the prize!" In his response, he was actually conveying to me that I was not worthy of him because of my decision of abstinence. In my response to him, I was actually conveying to him that *HE* was not worthy of me because he wasn't abstinent. I knew my worth and I was not settling for less. I hear you saying, "But if I chose abstinence then nobody would want me!" That's an emotional response based on fear and not love for one's self. Remember we must date by our standards and not by our emotions. A person who is Happily Single After Sexual Mishaps understands that her body is a prize to be won and not an item to be abused.

But Can I Test Drive?

A common question that comes to mind pertaining abstinence is, "How will I know sex will be good when I get married?" I ask you this. How will you know it will not be? The more a couple engages in sexual intercourse the more "average" it becomes. Contrary to popular belief you will not be "making love" with every session. That's a fairy tale we all need to wake up from! Why not save up that energy for your marriage? *Remember, you are building a foundation with a potential suitor and a part of this foundation is communication.* At the courtship stage of your relationship, it is important that you talk about your sexual expectations for marriage. When you get into your marriage, it will be imperative that you communicate your sexual needs and desires to your spouse and because you will have a strong foundation, your spouse will not be offended but you both will find ways to meet every need that the other has- including sexual needs. If you get married just for sex then your marriage has already failed. Eventually, a part won't work or an illness will come that will make sex difficult. *You have to marry with purpose in mind. Sex is temporal put purpose is everlasting.* A happy single is concerned with the everlasting and not just the here and now.

We carry a test drive mentality when it comes to sex. We want to try it out before we commit to that person. A car depreciates in value when you drive it off the lot. You are not a car so your value should appreciate and not depreciate. Often when we are "test driven" we cause an individual to miss out on our worth and the value we can add to their lives. You are worth so much more than what is between your legs! If their commitment to you is based solely upon sex and your abilities I would say that this is not the person for you. *Why would you want to be treated like something that loses value when your value is far beyond what you can comprehend?* You do not have to test drive when you are well acquainted with the Manufacturer (God).

Here's the truth. You have not officially bought a car until you sign the papers and drive it off the lot. Many men will not sign the papers (marriage) if you allow them to drive it off the lot beforehand. I remember dating a guy and he pursued sex. He was everything I wanted so I did what I thought would keep him. He then told me a few months later that he would never marry a woman that he slept with before marriage! Was I angry? YES! Did I call him a few choice words in my head? YES! But at the end of the day, I made a decision to lay with him and this did not pay off. The truth is that I viewed him as if he was everything I wanted and he was the prize but I did not look at myself as the prize I was or I would have waited until he truly "won" me. Most modern men will hit you with this line, "I won't think anything differently of you after we sleep together!" Then here we go as women (who date off emotions and not standards) believing what comes out of his mouth. We wonder why he never calls again or he suddenly starts to be inconsistent. It's because we let him test drive without the commitment to buy! A person who is Happily Single After understands that they are not to be test driven and that a potential suitor can only engage in sexual activity if they have purchased (signed the marriage papers) the total person.

Side Chick Mentality

Can I tell you a secret? You have to promise not to tell anyone. I have been a side chick more times than I'd like to mention. Now, don't judge me because I am sure you have been a side chick too. A side chick is simply a person who is used to being second or in a lower position. She doesn't know what it is like to be put first by a man so she settles for being second best. Yes, she *settles*! The side chick's motto is that it is better to have a piece of a man than no man at all. Women who sleep with married or unavailable men knowingly are classified as side chicks. Their impatience causes them to go down a road that leads to nowhere. To others, she is seen as desperate and needy. In her mind, she feels justified because life is taking too long to happen. The proper terminology for a side chick should probably be "Settling Chick" because she is not living up to the best life that she can have and has settled for the temporary mediocre thrill of the now.

Compromise is the gold standard of the side chick. Clocks and calendars govern the moves of a side chick because she feels her biological clock is ticking. This causes panic and rush and she now has a dilemma. Should she wait for this marriage that may never happen or should she get what she can for now and worry about the costs later? Sex is normally the first compromise that she makes. She has been taught that this is what all men want and because she has grown desperate she gives sex freely at the expense of herself.

A side chick is not always the home wrecker that we are accustomed to seeing. She can be the single mom who just needs "help" so she settles for a man who can provide for her financially, knowing that they have nothing else in common. She can be the traditional good girl with dreams of a marriage but she settles for a live-in man because she's afraid to lose him. A side chick can also be a person who settles for a man that's emotionally unavailable. She endures agony and defeat because she thinks that staying with him will "change" the nature of who he is. I have a question. Are you a side chick?

You are worth much more than being second best for anybody. A piece of man will always leave you in pieces. Abstinence without compromise puts your needs first. You have a need to be loved and cared for the way you always imagined and this is possible if you don't compromise. *When you settle, it will more than likely lead you down a path of pain, self-destruction, and misery. You will obtain attachments to a person who was never destined to go where you are going.* Then, years later, you will find yourself dealing with the reality of being a side chick. This compromise often causes you to miss your Prince Charming because the only potential he saw in you was side chick potential and not wife potential. He then moves on to find a Princess who is suited to be a wife. A person who is Happily Single After Sexual Mishaps understands that compromise is fatal to their destiny and they work hard to avoid it at any cost.

Sex is Free- But it Will Cost You!

In our hook-up culture, sex is readily available and easily accessible. No longer are dates with flowers and candy required before having sex but now sex is the reality of many first encounters. We jump in the bed before we jump in a person's head. We don't take the time to access the mental capacity or trustworthiness of a person and we can all agree that this cycle often lends itself to paying a lifetime for a moment of pleasure. This thing we call sex is free, but it will cost you!

I have paid many costs for sex. One of those costs is the fact that I have a severely shortened cervix due to treatment for HPV. I mentioned the cause of this in a previous chapter. I have spent thousands of dollars to recover and at one point the doctor considered performing a hysterectomy on me. There is nothing I desire more than being a mom one day and sex almost cost me my ability to ever experience motherhood. When I am married and conceive I will most likely have to get my cervix stitched just so my body can hold my child. Month after month I have had to see an oncologist to prevent the precancerous cells from turning into cancer. I have had one surgery and at least five procedures to maintain my fertility. I recently received a clean bill of health after years of enduring treatment after treatment. You may wonder why I am being so transparent about my costs. I want you to learn from my mistakes. If I don't tell my story you will never know that you can be victorious. There is no shame in my story because God has delivered, healed and freed me and you too can be free.

Beyond the physical costs of sex, there are additional costs. *Many times singles rush into sexual relationships without first establishing a friendship. As a result, a person who could have been a friend for life is now an enemy of strife.* This could be because the woman now falls pregnant and becomes a single parent when that wasn't initial her intent. It could also be because both parties feel ashamed of the act committed. Now they are paying the cost of having clouded vision by staying with a person they know isn't good for them but the sex was so good they can't let go. An addiction can now occur and the only way out is through prayer and counseling. You see, sex is free, but it will cost you!

Abstinence is a win-win situation. The only cost associated with abstinence is delayed gratification of your flesh. Can I be real with you? You are not that horny that you cannot wait. And in all honesty, if you are, there may be some hormonal issues that need to be addressed by a medical professional and the Holy Spirit. *The payoff for abstinence is that you know that a person wants to be with you for who you are and not for what you can offer them sexually. You will have mental clarity concerning the person because you will not be blinded by sex.* This makes it easier to see another person's flaws and consequently easier to cut them off if their flaws are beyond what you will accept. Abstinence increases your communication with your potential suitor because sex is often a result of boredom. When you take sex out of the equation then you find other ways to learn each other thus building a firm foundation. It also teaches you to control lust. If a person cannot control their lust before marriage, what would make you think that they would control their lust during your marriage? *If they can abstain with you then they have a greater likelihood of being committed to you after marriage.* Those who are Happily Single After Sexual Mishaps understand the importance of counting the cost before entering into a sexual relationship. They know that sex is free and the costs are not worth a lifetime of agony.

The Telegony Theory

One day a friend sent me a video of a woman speaking about what was known as the Telegony theory. This theory was introduced many years ago by Aristotle and it stated that a woman's offspring could be influenced by the previous men that she engaged in sexual intercourse with. It states that each man leaves a part of his DNA inside of the woman after sex and she carries his DNA for the remainder of her life. This DNA could cause her children to take on characteristics of her previous sex partners. After the sexual liberation movement, Telegony was said to be inaccurate and flawed because no one wanted to make women feel ashamed of their sexual escapades. Now, modern-day researchers are delving into the reality of Telegony to ascertain if this is truly occurring in human beings today.

Let's say for a moment that this theory is legitimate. What effects have our sexual partners had on our children or future children? Think about the last Bozo you slept with. What if your children have been specifically marked because of that encounter? Scary isn't it? Every time we have sex with a man we have the potential of creating a new life. You must ask yourself if this man is worth being called the patriarch of your family or is he only baby daddy potential. Even men have to ask if this woman is worthy to be called the matriarch of his family or if she is only baby mama potential. It's those quality decisions that can make the difference between you being Happily Single After or an Angry-Single-Parent After.

Sex is more than just a physical act as it includes your spirit, mind, and soul. Every time a woman engages in sexual intercourse with a man he leaves a certain part of him in her. She reciprocates by sharing a piece of her soul with each encounter. By nature, a woman is a receiver and a man is a giver. We physically receive what the man gives out. We receive his DNA and everything else he carries-from his emotions to his STD's. I am actually predisposed to agree with the Telegony theory for the simple fact that I believe that science can back up the Bible. When you understand the nature of soul ties, you can see how Telegony can be a reality.

Sex is driven by the limbic system in the brain. The limbic system is composed of complex nerves that deal with mood, and emotions such as fear, anger, and pleasure. It also deals with our sex and hunger drives. One of the functions of the limbic system is to also control our emotions related to sexual behavior. Understanding this function can help us to realize why the pleasure of sex can be addicting and why people, especially women, are likely to be emotionally attached after sexual encounters. The limbic system in females is actually bigger than the limbic system in males. This is why women cannot play the field sexually like men and expect there to be no emotional attachment or soul ties. We are biologically conditioned to think different, feel different, and act different. Can men have soul ties? Of course! However, this is a condition that is felt hardest by women due to the nature of our biological make-up. Soul ties are a reality whether we believe this or not. Let me give you a snippet of the reality of soul ties so that you can be the judge.

Tied Together

Have you ever left a relationship and found that it was hard to let go? Years later you are still thinking about the pain caused by the individual and as hard as you have tried you just can't seem to get over the person. Do you get a "jump" in the bottom of your stomach when you think about the individual with whom you once had a sexual encounter? Maybe you have found yourself thinking and acting like the person you had sex with. Are you currently in an abusive relationship and know full well that you need to get out but just can't find the strength to move forward? Maybe you are still clinging on to having a relationship with a person who has said that they do not want you. If you can answer yes to any of these then you, my friend, may have an ungodly soul tie!

Soul ties were designed by God as positive and nurturing connections. The first soul tie we encounter in the Bible is Adam and Eve. Eve was flesh of Adam's flesh and bone of Adam's bone. *They were one!* Soul ties can also occur among friends and associates such as David and Jonathan. Let's look at 1st Samuel 18:1.

"And it came to pass, when he had made an end of speaking unto Saul, that the soul of Jonathan was knit with the soul of David, and Jonathan loved him as his own soul."

Here we see a healthy emotional soul tie among friends. There was nothing shady or unnatural about this relationship. Godly soul ties are the type of soul ties husbands and wives should share. They are connected for a greater purpose. They are thinking the same and moving the same. When there is a Godly soul tie there is oneness with God. You feel a sense of wholeness and completion. Godly soul ties actually keep you on track with God because they are founded on love and not lust.

The problem with soul ties is that they are often perverted from God's original intent. This normally happens when we develop an emotional or sexual attachment to another person. *We develop these attachments because what we think is love turns out to be lust. How can we tell the difference between love and lust?* It's simple. Is your relationship primarily sexual in nature? If you told your current dating partner that you wanted to begin practicing abstinence would they agree or tell you that this is something they cannot deal with? 1st Corinthians 13:4-7 is the perfect description of love. It is not self-seeking but it makes sacrifices for the greater good of the relationship. *Lust looks like love until it's time to make a sacrifice.*

Ungodly soul ties are rooted in lust. They begin by looking like love but operate in the opposite of how God operates and causes separation from Him. Ungodly soul ties often end in brokenness and take individuals off their God-given path due to a deep attachment to the person who does not first yield to God's purpose. Let's look at the story of Shechem and Dinah in Genesis 34:2-3.

"And when Shechem the son of Hamor the Hivite, prince of the country, saw her, he took her and lay with her, and violated her. His soul was strongly attracted to Dinah the daughter of Jacob, and he loved the young woman and spoke kindly to the young woman."

Shechem's relationship with Dinah was rooted in lust. After this incident many issues were created. I will not delve into this but I make this point to say that anytime there is an ungodly soul tie, issues will be presented that go far beyond the two individuals involved. Ungodly soul ties cause dependency and depression because the thing that caused us pleasure (remember the limbic system) is now the thing that is causing us pain.

You Can be Free From Soul Ties!

After my breakup, I was still very attached to my ex. The attachment was probably the hardest part to get over. I realized that everything he was, I became. He was depressed and because of the soul tie, I became depressed. He was addicted to sex and drugs and after dealing with him I became addicted to food. *I needed this to break off of my life so that I could be free from the hurt and pain caused by the ending of the relationship.* I went through a process of deliverance and this is a process that you too can follow to be free from your soul tie. First, I had to ask for forgiveness because I was separated from God. I allowed my longing for a person to pull me off course with God. Secondly, I acknowledged that I gave the enemy access to my spirit through sex. When I acknowledged this I had to pray and ask God to block any spirits attached to me by the soul tie. I also removed everything in my possession I had that belonged to him. This way there were no physical attachments to possessions that could trigger the soul tie. Then I had to ask God to allow His Spirit to truly take over my life. Finally, I had to realize that I could not dip into sexual sin again. This would only have kept me bound to the soul tie and I would have to start the process all over again. Soul ties keep you in bondage and this is not the lifestyle of a happy single. A person who is Happily Single After Sexual Mishaps understands the importance of being released from ungodly soul ties because this person understands that bondage blocks blessings and hinders us from walking into our Happily Ever After!

How Can I be Abstinent?

The typical answer to the above question is to just not have sex but it's not that simple. You cannot stop a behavior without knowing how to channel it in a different direction. Often we are told to stop having sex but no one tells us how or if it is even possible. Take this from me. It is possible to lead an abstinent lifestyle. The keyword here is lifestyle. With any lifestyle change there are going to be steps that you must take to never go in the way of your old lifestyle again. For instance, as I am losing weight, I know that there are certain foods that I need to stay away from. I cannot indulge in sweets on a regular basis so I stay away from them as much as possible. I cannot hang with those who have an unhealthy lifestyle and gorge food because this will be a trigger for me and I cannot afford to go backward. Hopefully you are getting the picture and the parallel is adding clarity. I am going to give you a few pointers on how to be abstinent and stay abstinent until marriage.

Stay Busy- The best way that I have found to live an abstinent lifestyle is to stay busy. I am always doing something so I have little time to think about sex. A person who is Happily Single After Sexual Mishaps understands that an idle mind is truly the devil's workshop. This person finds time to socialize, work on their vision, and finds ways to improve their lifestyle for the better.

Be Accountable- Accountability allows another person to share in the standards you are holding yourself against. My best friend does what is called Suicide Watch. Suicide Watch is basically a code term that she uses when she feels like she wants to have sex. She calls her accountability partners (who are abstinent or married) for prayer and encouragement. She calls it Suicide Watch because she knows that she will literally kill everything she has been working hard to do just by engaging in sex. If your friends do not have an abstinent lifestyle then you may have to change your friendships. Find someone to whom you can be accountable or to whom you can be totally honest and transparent without judgment. Maybe you don't have this person in your life. Great! Start a group for those who want to be abstinent and run with it. You will be surprised to learn that more people have chosen abstinence or want to become abstinent but they just need your help in knowing how.

Make Abstinence a Core Value- As I mentioned in the previous chapter, one of the things I did with my relationship coach is set up a relational mission statement that was inclusive of my core values. Core values are non-negotiable traits in any man I date. I only have eight of them and one is abstinence. Any man I entertain has to be leading an abstinent life or willing to live this way to even be considered worthy of dating me. If I begin conversing with a man and he is not abstinent or if he is strongly sexual in his mannerisms, I instantly end all communication with him. Remember, you get a choice in who you date. You may think that there are no men that hold abstinence with high esteem. I will say that you need to change your company. There are more who are willing to practice it than you know. *The way to a man's heart is through the word "no" because he will always chase what he cannot have.*

Watch What You Watch- It will be difficult to live an abstinent lifestyle while watching movies that are sexually explicit- including pornography. These images totally defeat attempting to be abstinent because they cause imaginations and fantasies which will eventually lead to the act of sex. Movies today are full of sexual innuendos. There are times when you have to turn them off so that you can focus on your goal of abstinence. This also includes staring at semi-nude pictures of the opposite sex. A happy single understands that the eyes are the window to their soul and they guard what goes into their soul because eventually it will affect their spirit.

Think About What You Think About- Living an abstinent lifestyle is possible when you think on positive things. Philippians 4:8 tells us:

"...Fix your thoughts on what is true, and honorable, and right, and pure, and lovely, and admirable."

Our thought life can make or break us. As the scripture says, we have to concentrate on things that are pure. You cannot stop the birds (thoughts) from flying around your head, but you surely can stop them from building a nest! Control how long sexual thoughts are in your head. The way I do this is by recognizing the thought is impure. Then I start thinking of something else such as a song I like or my "To Do" list. Prayer is also a great strategy for controlling your thoughts. I don't know about you but I can't think about sex and God at the same time. If you allow those thoughts to fester then you will eventually fall into temptation. A person who is Happily Single After understands the importance of keeping their thought life in check and recognizes the consequences of letting their thought life run free.

Keep Boundaries with Dates- You are not a hermit so you will go out on dates. You may even begin dating a person or enter an exclusive courtship. It is very important that you keep boundaries in all of these situations. Be upfront from the very first conversation about your decision towards abstinence. This is not a time for you and that person to spend secluded time together. Public meetings always work best. It doesn't always have to cost money as there are coffee shops, parks, and museums that have free admission. This also gives you an opportunity to learn the other person outside of the bedroom.

You may be wondering how far is too far to go sexually and what boundaries you should keep. Some people chose not to hold hands or kiss before marriage. Others chose to hold hands and kiss with no other physical contact. *I can't tell you how far is too far for you. I will say that it is not how close you can come to the stove without getting burned but it is about having the wherewithal to know that even if you get close to the stove, the flames can still burn you.*

You must keep boundaries in what you talk about. I will not talk about sex with any man that I am not in the courtship stage with. Even in this stage the talk is not and will not be about what he wants to do to me sexually but it will be talk about the expectations of sex within the marriage. A particular man began telling me how physically attractive I was to him. Then he attempted to tell me what he wanted to do with me in the bedroom. I immediately shut him down before he could finish his sentence. Many times we are scared to shut them down because we don't want to come off as rude. *If he is the one for you then he will understand and respect your boundaries.* If not then he is an ungodly sexual soul tie waiting to happen. Even if you give a slight chuckle or a reply with a subtle "Boy Stop" this is a gateway to more sex talk. When a person only wants to talk about sex it should be a huge turn off because having conversations solely about sex is extremely juvenile. Children talk only about sex. Adults talk mostly about plans.

Remember, this is a day by day process. During this process, you may have some close calls. You may have days when you don't want to be accountable. You may have some days when you want to throw it all away. In these times remember why you made this decision. Remember your commitment to yourself. One moment of pleasure is not worth a lifetime of disappointment. When you have days like this, dust yourself off and start over again. Use positive affirmations when your mind drifts to negative thoughts. You are attempting to do something different so you have to always hold yourself accountable to truly being something different. Abstinence is not easy but it is worth it. A person who is Happily Single After does not beat themselves up because of slight mistakes. They take those mistakes and learn from them so that they won't repeat them ever again.

You can be single and not have sex. Is it easy? Nope! Is it doable? Yes! If the concept of giving up sex is mentally perplexing or you cannot fathom the idea of being sexually abstinent, you may seriously need to seek counseling from a trained professional. Sexual addiction is a real occurrence. *Anything you cannot master will eventually master you. A person who is Happily Single After understands that they are not mastered by anything except God.* They know that when there is control of their sexual life then all other areas will fall in line. You can do this! You can live free of the bonds of sex. Just take it one day and one step at a time. Your purpose will thank you for it!

Let Me Pray For You!

God I come thanking you for the person who is reading this and desires to be free from sexual mishaps. I pray that you will give them the strength and the power to overcome what has been holding them back. God please release her from the soul ties that have her bound. Please remove any attachment that is ungodly. We admit that we have made poor choices in this area but today we are free from the consequences of them. Thank you for letting us know that we never have to settle. We love you!

In Jesus' Name!

Amen!

Chapter Seven

Happily Single After Falling in Love with You

Most singles are looking for something so unique and so special. We want that person who is going to sweep us off our feet and make all of our dreams come true. We are looking for someone to love us- totally and unconditionally. In this book, we have dealt with the pain. We have dealt with our issues and dilemmas. There is just one more thing I want you to do before you exit this book. I want you to learn to love YOU!

Some time ago I remember sending a friend a text that said, "I HATE MYSELF!" I was in a very dry place and it seemed that there was no way out. Happiness was the last thing on my agenda. My weight ballooned due to emotional eating and my self-esteem was at an all-time low. I was fat, depressed and unhappy. I was at a point where I would rather die than to continue the life I had. You see, I'd had a difficult year prior, with the death of my father, a horrible breakup, canceled wedding, and aggressive treatment for pre-cancerous cells. To top that off I decided to buy my second home at the end of that year. After my old house was under contract and packed, the deal for the new house fell through. I was devastated and I could not comprehend why my life had been turned upside down. I allowed the events of my life to make me unhappy. I had two choices. I could stay where I was or make a decision to move forward and embrace happiness.

In 2016, I made a resolution to live my best life. I realized that the pain of my past left me assessing my worth based on my experiences. I challenged myself to take myself on 50 dates that year. I wanted to try different things alone and broaden my perspective on life. I embarked on what I called the "Journey to Self-Love." Another facet of this Journey for me was to attend counseling. Yes! Counseling. Sometimes the counselor needs counseling! It was great to have someone to share my feelings with in a nonjudgmental manner. During one of my visits, my counselor said the following words to me and it changed my life forever. **"YOU HAVE TO FALL IN LOVE WITH THE FAT GIRL!"** I wondered, "Who in the world wants to fall in love with a FAT GIRL??"

How could I fall in love with the fat girl? This fat girl is the one who naively stayed in a relationship with a man who cheated continuously and treated her like dirt. That fat girl was the one who did not speak to her father for four months before he passed. That fat girl was one who was shy and introverted. How could I fall in love with someone who had been taunted her whole life because of weight? How could I love the one they called "Fat-Cheska" in grade school?" Why would I love someone who used food as an emotional crutch to deal with the emotions of anger, hatred, and low self-esteem? What business would I have loving the one who was bankrupt by the age of 29? How could I fall in love with one who was 35, never married, and had no kids? Why would I love someone as imperfect as the FAT GIRL? How could I fall in love with her when she was EVERYTHING that I hated? You see, that FAT GIRL was me!

The truth was life changing. I had to find a way to fall in love with the part of me that I hated. At this point my self-confidence was low and at times my will to live was on a short fuse. My focus began to change and I begin to think on the good things that this FAT GIRL had accomplished. She was the one who basically put herself through college. She was the one who bought a home at 25 and still has that home today. She was the one who obtained a

Master's degree and had a successful career as an educator. She obtained a Certification as a Belief Therapist and created the Raising Our Self EsteemS (ROSES) organization. That FAT GIRL was a Licensed and Ordained Elder who has had the opportunity to minister to thousands. I had to find a way to fall in love with the great things about her- and I did.

You see, you, too, may need to fall in love with the FAT GIRL. Maybe your FAT GIRL is not an actual FAT GIRL. Your FAT GIRL represents your flaws. Maybe your flaw is that you are a recovering drug addict. Maybe your flaw is that you served time in prison. Whatever your FAT GIRL is, you have to find it within yourself to fall in love with her. How do you do that? Good Question! You do that by changing your focus. Too many times we are overly harsh on ourselves and we don't celebrate the person we have become. Falling in love with you means spending time ALONE to find out the good, bad, and ugly about who YOU really and truly are. Your past and your flaws are a part of you. You would not be who you are without them. We must embrace the reality of our flaws so we can enjoy the promise of our future. Today, you must fall in love with the FAT GIRL and watch how she allows you to live Happily Single After!

Self-love is best defined as regard for one's own well-being and happiness. *It is not a narcissistic act where you only love you or that your complete focus is on yourself but it is about being the best you possible. Self-love does not take away from your love for God nor does it mean that you are better than anyone else.* The Bible warns against this type of self-love as 1st Timothy 3:1-2 speaks about how men will be lovers of themselves in the last days. This type of self-love comes from a place of arrogance and is not the type of self-love I am describing in this chapter. Self-love is you accepting yourself fully and focusing on the positives over the negatives. There are a few signs that you are not operating in this self-love. The first sign is that you cannot fully say that you love yourself. Secondly, you are not operating in self-love when you make the same relationship mistakes over and over. Maybe you don't have love for yourself because you stay in abusive relationships due to low self-esteem. Also, a person who practices self-hate does not care about their grooming or appearance. They focus more on their negative attributes and are often victims of self-fulfilling prophecies. Lastly, those who operate in self-hate put others down in order to make themselves seem bigger. Have you identified yourself in any of these situations or similar? If so you may not be walking in self-love.

Franceska M. Price

You may say that you don't have time to love yourself because you are so busy taking care of other people. That's wonderful but it reminds me of riding on a plane. When safety instructions are being given passengers are told that in case of an emergency they need to put on their oxygen mask before helping their neighbor put on theirs. Why is this? The airlines know that you cannot be of any assistance to others if you are in need of assistance. You cannot save another person until you learn to save you. A happy single understands that they must let go of all instances of self-hate and fall in love with the person they are today.

You may be in a situation where you feel all hope is gone. You may be in an unhappy place. Maybe you have just left a relationship where your partner has told you that you were unworthy and you didn't deserve to be loved. *I want to encourage you today to find your joy! Do you really and truly love you? Can you say at the end of the day that you totally and completely love the person you are today?* A person who is happily single understands that no one can love you properly unless you first love yourself. You teach people how to treat you. When you do not love yourself, you cannot teach others how to love you properly simply because you have never learned how you need to be loved. The only way you can be Happily Single After is by unlocking the beauty within you to realize that there is a hidden treasure deep inside! Here are a few ways happy singles find happiness and truly fall in love with who they are.

Happy Singles Don't Depend on Anyone Else for Happiness.

One day I asked a male associate if he was in a "happy" place in life. He told me that he wasn't because he did not have a wife or children. My words to him were that I, too, could use a lack of husband or children as an excuse to not be happy. His desire to receive the validation that comes from having a family shielded him from experiencing happiness in his everyday single life. *The truth is your happiness does not depend on another person and their validation. Happiness is a result of your inward thoughts and motivations.* Be careful of people who say "YOU MAKE ME HAPPY" or even when you tell someone that they make you happy. Will you be unhappy once they stop doing the things that make you happy? What will be the end result when this happens? If you are dependent on another for happiness you have come to your first downfall.

At one point in my life, my worth was defined by my experiences. I believed that I was worthless because

I was treated like I was worthless. When my ex and I parted ways, I remember how the prostitute he slept with told me how he was not attracted to me. This weighed on my heart heavily because I had never been called unattractive and the person I looked to the most for confidence felt that I wasn't. Did you read that last line carefully? The person I looked to the most for confidence! I allowed a prostitute and a manipulator to define my personal worth. Some of you are in the same situation. You have allowed a person who does not know your character to define your life. You have stopped loving who you are because someone has told you that you aren't worth it. *Your experiences with others do not signify your worth!* Yes, negative things happened but your life is not the sum total of the things that happened. A person who is Happily Single After understands the importance of self-validation. When you are happily single you know that your worth is based solely on who you are and not other people's opinion of you.

Happy Singles are Thankful.

Too often, we focus on what we don't have- like the gentleman did above. I haven't obtained this spot in my career. I haven't earned this amount of money. Let me challenge you. What *have* you accomplished? What has God done for you lately? What are you truly thankful for? *Thankfulness breaks the back of depression and self-hate.* When I could not love myself, I had to focus on the things in which I excelled. Happy Singles spend 5-10 minutes every morning thinking about those things that are positive in their lives. Challenge yourself to do this daily. I bet your entire being will change!

Happy Singles are Happy on Purpose.

When we are not fulfilling our purpose we will never be happy. What is that business you are supposed to start? What is that endeavor you are supposed to embark upon? I am best fulfilled when I am serving others. Could the reason why you are so unhappy be because you have an assignment by God and you are sitting on it? You will never find fulfillment outside of the will of God. Are you in a relationship that is not purpose ordained? This is not just about intimate relationships but it could be friendships and associations. If so, it may be time to remove yourself from that situation and find purpose. You were designed to be so much more than an unhappy single. You were designed to rule and dominate. You, my friend, were designed to walk in purpose. Purpose creates happiness!

Self-love comes on the hinge of walking in purpose. When you walk in purpose you become who you were destined to be. I remember giving up preaching because I felt that it was burdensome and that no man would ever want to date a female preacher. I walked out of my purpose and I began to be a person that I did not even recognize. Depression set in and as a result self-hate was my coping mechanism. Something in my life was missing and broken. I found that I missed training leaders and teaching the Word of God. I needed to quickly get back to being the person I was destined to be. When I connected back with my purpose, my entire life changed and my love for me went to new levels. A person who is Happily Single After Falling in Love with Themselves knows that self-love comes on the wings of walking in their purpose.

Happy Singles are Transparent with People in Their Lives.

Happy singles understand that proper communication is essential in any relationship. They do not shy away from conflict nor do they hold in their feelings concerning another. As a happy single, you must know that if you allow issues to linger then these issues will become like cancer and spread internally while causing a metaphoric death to everything it encounters. Often, we hold in our feelings towards others for fear of damaging the other person. There comes a time when you have to release these feelings in a positive and productive manner. You cannot be a happy single while holding on to conflict with others.

Many of us need to do what I call a transfer of emotions. A transfer of emotions is simply when you express your feelings to another person. These can be feelings of anger, unhappiness, grievances, or even joy caused by another. When you transfer your emotions you allow the other person to share in how you feel. Think about the last time you had a grievance against someone and you held onto it. How did it make you feel internally? How did it change your opinion of them? You probably replayed the situation over and over and had emotional distress for weeks, months, and even years. A transfer of emotions is about immediately expressing how you feel to others. This allows YOU to feel better. We often regard other's feelings more than our own. YOU HAVE A RIGHT TO YOUR FEELINGS! *A transfer of emotions is more about "unloading" so that the load and pressure of the offense are removed from you and it allows the other person to be accountable for their actions- good or bad.* They become accountable because they are now aware of any emotions you may feel as a result of an action by them.

When you transfer emotions you simply allow the other person to hear you out and you are not holding on to feelings of discord. You have to be prepared to not receive the answer that you want but to be prepared to get the answer the person is ready to give. For example, one day I was on a conference call with some leaders from church. I had an idea that I thought would move the church forward. I felt extremely attacked by the individuals and I cried the entire call unbeknownst to them. I would traditionally hold in these feelings or text about how I felt but this time I held a one to one conversation with the primary offender and as a result, I allowed the leader to feel some of the offense that I felt. Did I cry through that conversation? Of course! But at the end of the day, I was cleansed of ill will and feelings towards that individual.

A transfer of emotions does not come from a place of anger but it is about having civil conversations to come to a resolve on an issue. There are people in your life that you need to have an honest transfer of emotions with. You need to express the joy, the hurt and the pain to them so that you can move forward in happiness. Do that NOW!! A person who is Happily Single After understands the importance of communication with those in their life and uses this to help them reach their ultimate state of happiness.

Happy Singles Commit to Self-Improvement.

I am a firm believer that if you don't like something about yourself you get up and change it! If you want to be a better person you be that. Happy singles don't make excuses about where they are in life but they get up and make things happen. You have to commit to self-improvement daily. What's the number one area in your life that you hate? What changes are you making in that area? Someone recently complained to me about their weight. They said, "I can't work out because I am busy." Busy people work out every day! Our problem is that we have an "exclusivity" mindset. We think that we are exclusively the only person in life who has ever gone through a situation. You know this is your mindset when you see people in your same situation and start making excuses such as, "Well she can do that because she has help," or "He got that job because of who he knows and I can never get a job like that because I don't know anyone." *Listen, what is for you is for you and no one can take that away from you but YOU!*

Many of you have used your children as an excuse. You feel you can't travel because of them or you can't go back to school because your children need you. The reality is that your children need to see you engaged in the true essence of being the best you that you can possibly be. They need to know that excuses are not an option but that you can do and achieve anything you set your mind to. You are not the first single parent to go through what you are going through and you won't be the last.

I currently live in Houston, Texas and it is a huge melting pot. I wanted to learn to speak Spanish because of the plethora of Hispanics in this area. I took all excuses out of the way and began to take Spanish classes. I was unhappy with my body so I took a trip to Mexico and had a Vertical Sleeve Gastrectomy (gastric sleeve) which has helped me to lose weight. As my body changed I noticed I did not like how my body sagged so I started to take Pilates and exercise. I hold a full-time job and I am extremely active in ministry along with other personal endeavors. I could have used every excuse in the book to stop my transformation but I wanted it more than anything. You have to want to improve more than you want to stay in your current situation. *Think of it as an investment into yourself. You will only get out what you put in. This is an investment that can reap huge amounts of interest. I am no better than you. If I can self-improve, so can you!* A person who is Happily Single After knows that self-improvement is the gateway to self-love.

Happy Singles are Not People Pleasers.

This section doesn't need a lot of words. Listen, you cannot make others happy! It is their job to make them happy and it is your job to ensure you are happy. When they see that YOU are happy with you then they will have no choice but to be happy with you. You define your own space and you live in that space. You cannot be Happily Single After Falling in Love with You if you are still holding on to the idea of making everyone in your life happy. *Misery loves company and while you are on the road to learning to love yourself others won't be happy because they are enjoying living in their dysfunction. Do it anyway! Love you anyway!* Yes, people will talk about you but guess what? They are talking about you anyway, so why not allow them to talk about the positive changes you are making. *You do not need anyone's permission to be happy! God has given you that permission. It's time to walk in it.*

Happy singles also fight daily against being a perfectionist. They understand that being a perfectionist is a part of pleasing people and this is a space they cannot afford to live in. You will never be perfect in every single task that you do. With this perfectionism, we often allow others to throw guilt towards us as singles. They say, "Well you don't have kids so why don't you have money saved?" Others may say, "Since you are single you have it easier." As singles, we begin to hear these things and feel a measure of guilt because we know the hard work we put into life daily. We may be tempted to work harder to prove others wrong but it is important to not give in to that temptation. Happy singles continue on their grind despite the inaccuracies of others. They don't worry about being perfect, they focus on getting better.

Happy Singles Pray!

Happy singles know that they need regular communication with God to maintain their happiness. Prayer is simply communication with God. If you are a believer in Christ, it is imperative for your prayer life to be on point. *When we are disconnected from God unhappiness can set in. Contrary to popular belief, you do not have to wake up at 5 a.m. to pray or pray for hours at a time. God rewards effort! You can talk to God whenever and where ever. He wants to hear from you but most importantly He wants to talk to you.* There are some areas in your life that you cannot conquer without the love of God and the guidance of the Holy Spirit. Prayer demonstrates your love for

Him and allows Him to demonstrate His love back to you. This brings a closeness and intimacy that you have never known. In this closeness with Him, you will discover who you are and when you discover who you are this is the place of ultimate happiness!!

A Final Note about Happiness

As a single person, you can have it all! You CAN be SINGLE AND HAPPY! You were made in the image and reflection of God. You were made to rule. Affirm yourself daily with the word of God. *Wake up every morning and declare that you will praise God because you are fearfully and wonderfully made.* You were not meant to live some average and mundane single life but you were meant to live in abundance as a single. A spouse will not make you happy if you are not already happy when you encounter them. A new job won't make you happy if you are not happy from within. *Happiness is an INSIDE job. It starts in your mind, is expressed in your words, and is made manifest by your actions.*

Today I need you to experience a HOP! What is a HOP? A HOP is <u>Happiness On Purpose</u>! You must be intentional about your happiness. You must also realize that your happiness does not come by way of making others unhappy or taking a "slipper" that was designed to be worn by another. You are happy when you are in your own lane and driving your own car. Your happiness cannot come if you are living in a state of separation from God. A person who is Happily Single After understands that to love one's self requires a deeper commitment to others and God and they commit to love no matter what the situation may bring. You can be single and happy. Own it. Walk in it. Embody it!

Let Me Pray For You!

Father, we thank you that you are a Good Father and that you love us even when we don't love ourselves. Teach us to love us and others more and more daily. Show us areas where we need to experience self-improvement. Help us to fall in love with prayer. We know that we cannot truly love ourselves if we do not truly love you because we were created to love you. Today remind my brother and my sister that they are fearfully and wonderfully made in your image. We love you and we are learning to love ourselves more and more daily. Thank you for being our example and teacher.

In Jesus' Name!

Amen!

After ...

You can be single and happy. It pains me to hear singles complain about how boring single life is or how they desperately want a spouse. This lets me know that they are not maximizing their time as a single person but they are sitting back waiting for a fairy tale to unfold. *Happy singles create their own fairy tales. They do not sit back and wish that things will happen, they get up and make things happen.*

One of my goals in writing this book was to not pacify you. I did not want to shield you from the harsh reality that singleness can cause. My goal was to be straightforward with you so that you can rise above your current circumstances and recognize the true blessing of singleness. A person who is Happily Single After embraces these circumstances and uses them as a push in the right direction.

We must do our best to maximize our time as singles. This includes taking financial courses and budgeting correctly. Maximize your credit score and work extra jobs to pay off debt. Travel should be standard for you in your time of singleness. Join travel groups and plan a trip every summer. Take a dance or even cooking classes. Go back to school and get the degree you always wanted. Stop making excuses! *Our singleness is a time to develop into a well-rounded or whole person. When you walk into your Happily Ever After, you should be complete and very little should be missing from your life.*

Misery loves company. If you wish to maintain your status as a happy single, you must be in the company of other happy singles. Join support groups online that are geared towards helping singles be happily single. You can even join our Happily Single After group on Facebook for feedback and advice or even contact us about our yearly summer single's retreat. Begin to seek out like-minded people who are moving in the same direction as you. *Misery often comes when we begin gazing at marriage instead of focusing on being a happy single.* While there is nothing wrong with preparing for marriage singles must keep their concentration on maximizing the time given. If marriage is your desire, know that God will provide this for you but there are some things that you have to do first. That includes capitalizing on your time as a single person.

There are no excuses or shortcuts in life. Refuse to sit back and compare your life to another person. Just because you have children does not mean that you cannot maximize your single life. Your kids actually need to see you taking care of yourself. Just because your finances are not what you desire doesn't mean you can't achieve greatness. There are free resources available to you if you just search for them. *Take risks to become the person you've always wanted to be. You can no longer play it safe. Try a new hairstyle or find a new hobby. Singlehood is not about excuses, but it's all about action.*

We all have an after! Maybe your after did not turn out the way you thought it should be. There is good news! You decide how your after is going to look from this point forward. Will you sit in misery because the life you planned is not the life you are experiencing or will you get up and make the best out of your life as you know it? You cannot change what has happened before but you can change what will happen after! God is writing your unique love story. Trust Him with the pen!

FOR ADDITIONAL RESOURCES OR TO REACH THE
AUTHOR FOR SPEAKING ENGAGEMENTS, BOOK CLUBS,
OR PERSONAL COACHING/BELIEF THERAPY CONTACT:

Francheska M. Price

Website: www.francheskaprice.com

E-mail: francheskamprice@gmail.com

Facebook: @francheskamprice

Instagram, Periscope, Twitter: @francheskaprice

Made in the USA
Coppell, TX
18 October 2022